KUMBHA

The Ageless Tradition of Ascetics, Mystics, Culture, and Beyond

Mayur Pandey

KUMBHA

Publisher: Notion Press Media Pvt. Ltd.
7, Red Cross Road, Egmore, Chennai, Tamil Nadu—600008, India

Author: Mayur Pandey
9E/1A, Liddle Road
Website: George Town, Prayagraj – 211002
www.sahityawala.com

First Edition: 2025
Cover Design: Sahityawala Team
ISBN: 979-8897244065

For permissions or inquiries, please contact:
sahityawala.team@gmail.com

Kumbha is a work of thought and imagination that interweaves history, philosophy, and reflection. It does not claim to be a final or definitive account; rather, it is an offering meant to provoke inquiry, invite dialogue, and encourage debate. The references and interpretations presented here are intended as starting points for readers to engage, question, and explore further. Agreement or disagreement with the ideas expressed is part of the spirit in which this work has been written.

Dedicated

"To the Śrāut Smārta Ṛṣi
Paramparā, a lineage of eternal
knowledge and spiritual
wisdom, of which Devarṣi
Nārad is the true embodiment."

KUMBHA

Mañgalācharaṇ

1. आ नो भद्राः क्रतवो यन्तु विश्वतः।

   (Ṛk Saṁhitā 1.89.1)
   Let noble thoughts come to me from all directions.

2. सच्चिदानन्दरूपाय प्रत्ययात्मस्वरूपिणे।
   नित्याय विभुरूपाय सर्वरूपाय ते नमः॥

   To the one whose form is Sat (existence), Chit (consciousness), and Ānanda (bliss), and who is the very essence of inner consciousness and realisation; to the eternal being, unchanging through time, transcendent of spatial limitations, and manifest in all forms—I offer my salutations.

Contents

Preface

Developing a narrative is crucial for both novelists and non-fiction writers. One must understand the unforeseen circumstances that inevitably arise during an author's journey. A new fact, a new detail, or even the smallest thought of change can lead to significant differences. At times, the set narrative takes an unexpected turn, resulting in outcomes far better than originally envisioned. However, there are also moments when even the most well-constructed narratives lack the momentum to be expressed fully, leaving them unarticulated and lost in the forge of creation. It could be taken as the first challenge.

This experience is shared by everyone who has ever held a pen to write. Words are shy by nature; they do not come when called. They hide themselves. Only when one becomes an admirer of words do they reveal themselves. If neglected, they retreat once more to the realm from which they manifested. Thus, the second challenge lies in exercising care and patience.

In the making of this book, ***Kumbha: The Ageless Tradition of Ascetics, Mystics, Culture, and Beyond***, the set narrative unfolded differently than anticipated. Yet, these deviations often produced results far better than imagined.

Bhartṛhari, in his Vākyapadīya, observed:

न सोऽस्ति प्रत्ययो लोके यः शब्दानुगमाद्ऋते।
अनुविद्धमिव ज्ञानं सर्व शब्देन भासते॥
(Vākyapadīya 1.123)

> **Meaning:** "There is no cognition in the world in which the word does not figure. All knowledge is, as it were, intertwined with the word."

What he said is profoundly true. Even the subtlest thoughts require words to be fully expressed. Words carry meanings that are inseparably linked to them. The śruti affirms that words and their meanings are as inseparable as Śiva and Śakti.

The Rudrahṛdayopaniṣad beautifully expresses this oneness:

रुद्रोऽर्थ अक्षर: सोमा तस्मै तस्यै नमो नम: ।

रुद्रो लिङ्गमुमा पीठं तस्मै तस्यै नमो नम: ॥

(Rudrahṛdayopaniṣad 23)

> **Meaning:** Rudra signifies the Artha (meaning); Akṣara (letter) signifies Umā. To both, I bow. Rudra is the liṅga (form), and Umā is the pīṭha (base). To both, I bow.

This verse emphasises the unity of Rudra and Umā as word and meaning, inseparable and interdependent. Just as Śiva and Śakti are one, words and their meanings are intertwined, manifesting as the inseparable liṅga and pīṭha. This sacred unity inspires the understanding that all knowledge and expression originate from the profound relationship between words and their inherent meanings.

When words are chosen and used thoughtfully, they carry great energy and serve as powerful tools for expressing the deepest emotions of consciousness. Their effectiveness depends on careful, deliberate use to ensure they accurately convey intended meanings and preserve the essence of the thoughts they express.

The idea of expression comes from the soul or Ātmā and is articulated through the coordination of various parts of the subtle and physical body. The navel (nābhi), mind (manas), pharynx (kaṇṭha), hard palate (tālu), soft palate (mūrdhan), teeth (dantāḥ), nose (nāsikā), and lips (oṣṭhau), these eight organs work together to transform thoughts into reality and express them. They collaborate harmoniously to produce the different sounds of speech.

As the Laghusiddhānta-Kāmudī explains:

अकुहविसर्जनीयानां कण्ठः। इचुयशानां तालुः। ऋटुरषाणां मूर्धा। लुतुलसानां दन्ताः। उपूपध्मनीयानामोष्ठौ। अमङ्णनानां नासिका। एदैतोः कण्ठतालु। ओदौतोः कण्ठोष्ठम्। वकारस्य दन्तोष्ठम्। नासिकाऽनुस्वारस्य। **(Sañjña Prakaraṇ, 1.1.9, commentary)**

Thus, we now understand that words are the most critical aspect of any expression. The ability of any being in this universe to communicate is rooted in the inseparable, eternal coexistence of words and their meanings.

शान्तं शिवमद्वैतम्। **(Māṇḍūkyopaniṣad 7)**
एकं शिवं शान्तमनंतमच्युतं ब्रह्म। **(Kālīkā Purāṇa 13.48)**
ब्रह्मशक्तिरेव प्रकृतिः। **(Niralambopaniṣad)**

According to Vedāntic philosophy, Śiva is Brahman, the ultimate reality, and Śakti is his power, Prakṛti. The universe exists because of its indivisible unity. In this context, the universe itself can be seen as the cosmic literature (Sāhitya) of Śiva and Śakti, an eternal and divine expression of their oneness.

Thus, the universe is the literature of Śiva and Śakti, just as this book is the literature of words and meanings. By the Rudrahṛdayopaniṣad verse mentioned above, both are, in essence, one. This literature, like all others, is ultimately an offering to the Divine—the eternal being whose form is Sat (existence), Chit (consciousness), and Ānanda (bliss), the very essence of inner consciousness and realisation. To this timeless and transcendent presence, manifest in all forms, I dedicate this work.

The idea of writing about Kumbha came to me while travelling through Prayāgarāj and observing the remarkable developments in the city. As someone born and raised in Prayāgarāj, the town that hosts Kumbha—the world's largest spiritual gathering, I felt an innate connection to this subject. Kumbha, revered as the planet's most significant festival, inspired me to delve deeper into its various dimensions. This book, encompassing the essential aspects of Kumbha, is a humble offering to the Śraut-Smārta Ṛṣi Paramparā, the lineage of eternal knowledge and spiritual wisdom.

I have always viewed Indian traditions from an inherently Indian perspective, which has allowed me to understand them as they have existed for thousands of years. In contrast, foreign travellers, though they offer valuable insights, often interpret what they observe through their cultural lens, which is inevitably shaped by the traditions of their homeland. One such example is Pān, or the betel leaves, which, although a common and integral part of daily life in India, tends to be overlooked by the people themselves. However, foreign observers, such as Al-Biruni, would take note of such customs and record them in their writings, drawing attention to aspects of our culture that we, perhaps, do not even consider significant. For instance, in Northern India, Pān is traditionally prepared with a variety of ingredients, while in the South, coconut plays a more prominent role. Yet, to an outsider, such details would be fascinating and noteworthy.

This approach, although it may overlook some aspects that are more evident to others, is fundamentally ethnic, rooted in the belief that we all perceive the world through the lens of what is meaningful to us. As human beings, we naturally focus on those elements of life that resonate with us the most. This phenomenon is captured in the philosophy of Syādvād, which suggests that a single entity can have an infinite number of perspectives and that we can never fully grasp the complete truth. However, even if we only understand one perspective of India's rich culture and tradition, it would be a remarkable achievement. Through this book, I offer my attempt to bring this great tradition into the light, recognising that many have contributed to it in more profound ways before me. While my work may seem like a repetition of what has already been done, I believe that each individual must contribute in their unique way. My contribution, through writing, is my way of honouring our culture, without any expectation of reward—simply as an offering to my motherland. And so, this book becomes the first flower I offer in gratitude to the traditions that have shaped me.

The title ***Kumbha: The Ageless Tradition of Ascetics, Mystics, Culture, and Beyond*** encapsulates a broad spectrum of themes explored throughout the book. Each term in the title and subtitle reflects the rich and multifaceted nature of the Kumbha Melā. Below is a brief overview of these terms and their significance:

KUMBHA

1. **Kumbha:** The Kumbha refers to the sacred gathering held at four prominent locations in India, Haridwar, Prayagraj, Nashik, and Ujjain, during specific planetary alignments. These celestial arrangements imbue the land with heightened sanctity, offering devotees opportunities to attain both spiritual and material blessings. Participation in Kumbha is believed to purify one's karmas, attract auspiciousness, and enhance the pursuit of a dhārmik life, thereby fostering a path toward liberation.

2. **The Ageless Tradition:** Kumbha is an ancient tradition that spans time immemorial, mentioned in various Purāṇas and historical records. It has crossed the boundaries of time, with references in the accounts of Chinese traveller Xuánzàng (Hiuen Tsang), who observed its occurrence in Prayāgrāj, Haridwār, Nāsik, and Ujjayunī. The literary mentions, coupled with archaeological evidence, establish Kumbha as one of the oldest cultural gatherings on Earth— alive, vibrant, and youthful to this day.

3. **Ascetics:** The essence of Kumbha is incomplete without its ascetics, who have renounced worldly life to pursue salvation and liberation from the cycle of birth and death. As Ādi Śaṅkarācārya aptly expressed:

पुनरपि जननं पुनरपि मरणं पुनरपि जननी जठरे शयनम्।
इह संसारे बहु दुस्तारे कृपयाऽपारे पाहि मुरारे॥ [1]

This eternal cycle, central to Indian ascetic philosophy, inspires ascetics to gather at Kumbha

---

[1] *Reference: Śloka of Bhaj Govindaṁ composed by Ādi Śaṅkarāchārya.*

to perform sacred rituals. Organised into Akhāḍās, these groups of ascetics uphold the traditions of spiritual knowledge and the path of mokṣa. Some also live as individual practitioners affiliated with specific sampradāyas.

The Akhāḍās are not merely congregations of ascetics; they are custodians of dharma, offering guidance and support to the spiritual and cultural fabric of society. They conduct various saṃskāras, such as group marriages and mass yajñopavīta ceremonies, while also providing military and moral support to protect culture and religion. Historically, their unwavering commitment has preserved dharma during times of adversity. Beyond spiritual contributions, ascetics also enhance societal welfare through acts of service, including Gau Sewā (cow protection), Bhaṇḍāras (free food distribution), and other charitable activities. Their involvement extends to fostering economic and cultural growth, demonstrating their vital role in sustaining the spiritual and material well-being of society.

This interplay of asceticism, service, and cultural preservation highlights the profound significance of ascetics within the Kumbha Melā and the broader Indian traditions.

4. **Mystics:** Mystics stand alongside ascetics in the Kumbha, embodying the spirit of devotion and faith. By mystics, I refer to the countless devotees who journey to the Kumbha sites for sacred practices such as snān (ritual bathing), dhyān (meditation), dān (charitable giving), vrat (ritual fasting), and tīrthāṭan (pilgrimage). These pilgrims come to worship, seek blessings, and listen to the profound sermons of sādhus and saints. The Kumbha offers them a unique

opportunity to immerse themselves in a spiritually charged environment, living entirely by dhārmik means. This not only helps them attain a sense of inner purity and spiritual merit but also inspires personal growth and transformation, enabling them to return as better individuals, enriched by the wisdom of the saints' teachings.

5. **Culture:** Kumbha, celebrated for its spiritual and religious significance, has had a profound influence on the culture of the Indian subcontinent. Its deep roots in religious and historical texts have inspired countless traditions, leaving an indelible mark on Indian art, literature, and heritage.

   Kumbha's cultural prominence is highlighted in historical accounts by foreign travellers such as Fa Hien and Xuánzàng, who documented its grandeur in their writings. Xuánzàng noted that during the Kumbha and Ardha Kumbha festivals, King Harṣa would distribute all his wealth as dān (charity), showcasing the festival's unparalleled spiritual and social influence.

   The Kumbha's cultural significance extends beyond religion, symbolising the unity and collective identity of Indian society. Its recognition as an "Intangible Cultural Heritage of Humanity" by UNESCO further underscores its global cultural and historical importance.

6. **Beyond:** The term "Beyond" in the title reflects the broader spectrum of aspects that Kumbha encompasses, which could not be explicitly included. It represents an appreciation of the festival's historicity, showcasing its deep roots in the annals of time and its enduring legacy. It also signifies the geographical importance of the

sacred locations that host the Kumbha, underscoring their unique spiritual and cultural resonance. Moreover, it acknowledges the significant economic impact of this grand congregation, as well as its profound connection to nature and the environment, emphasising sustainability and ecological harmony.

Thus, the title, along with its inherent meaning and intention, has been briefly explained. With this foundation laid, let us now take a concise look at the chapters and their subject matter, offering a glimpse into the rich heritage of India explored within them.

1. **Kumbha: An Introduction**
   The introduction to Kumbha highlights its cultural and spiritual significance, extending beyond a mere religious gathering. The festival is rooted in ancient practices, which are observed meticulously, even in the absence of modern technology. The Kumbha Melā's unique convergence of time, place, and celestial configurations brings people together, irrespective of caste or status. This inclusivity and profound faith draw millions to the sacred event, emphasising the transformative power of collective devotion. The words of Mahātmā Gāndhī encapsulate this essence, illustrating Kumbha's role in fostering spiritual purity and national unity.

2. **Kumbha: Vaidik and Purāṇic References**
   Chapter 2 of Kumbha explores Vaidik and Purāṇic references to Kumbha, which symbolises spiritual prosperity, purity, and

the quest for immortality. In the Mahābhārata, Kumbha is associated with the essence of life and the pursuit of liberation (mokṣa). Vaidik texts mention Kumbha as a pot filled with nectar or soma, symbolising the divine and eternal life. The Atharva Veda and Purāṇas emphasise its role in rituals and its association with prosperity. The Kumbha festival, celebrated at four holy sites, embodies the pursuit of Dharma, Artha, Kāma, and Mokṣa, offering spiritual benefits to participants.

3. **Kumbha: Story as in Purāṇas**
Building upon the textual references, this chapter explores the stories of Kumbha as narrated in the Puranas, Mahabharata, and other ancient texts. It examines two principal narratives of the origin of Kumbha, highlighting their divergence due to Kalpbhed (differences in cosmic epochs). These stories are analysed in light of their scriptural references, paving the way for a deeper understanding of their embedded philosophical meanings.

4. **Kumbha: A Philosophical Insight**
. This chapter continues by delving into the philosophical dimensions of Kumbha. Rooted in the Vaidik and Paurāṇic traditions, every story or concept is understood on three levels: Adhibhūt (material aspect), Adhidaiv (divine aspect), and Ādhyatm (spiritual aspect). Here, the festival, the term 'Kumbha,' its symbols, and metaphors are analysed for their profound philosophical significance,

enriching the reader's appreciation of its deeper meanings.

5. **Kuṁbha: An Analysis of Jyotiṣa**
. After the philosophical insights have been described in all their significance, we move toward the astronomical and astrological aspects of the festival. This chapter explores the celestial configurations that determine the timing of Kuṁbha. It reveals how the festival aligns with the geometric coordination of the planets within the solar system, the rāśīs (zodiacs), and other cosmic factors. A particularly noteworthy aspect is the pivotal role of Bṛhaspati (Jupiter) in determining the festival's occurrence. The 12-year interval between Kuṁbha celebrations corresponds to the time it takes for Bṛhaspati to complete one revolution around the sun. This synchronisation not only adds a scientific dimension to the festival but also underscores the advanced astronomical understanding of ancient Indian scholars. The precise alignment of these calculations with modern scientific knowledge highlights the brilliance of Indian tradition and its profound grasp of cosmic phenomena.

6. **Kuṁbha: Historical Perspective**
Following the historical importance of Kuṁbha, this chapter examines the evolution of Kuṁbha as a melā (fair), congregation, and its transformation through the ages. The origins of Kuṁbha, shrouded in antiquity, may have started as a small social or spiritual gathering that

gradually evolved. However, due to various invasions of Indian institutions and inevitable natural factors, much of the ancient documentation of the early structure of Kumbha has been lost. This presents a challenge for modern historians and researchers attempting to trace its origins.

Notable foreign travellers have described Kumbha as a grand festival. Xuánzàng, for instance, recorded how King Harṣa gave away all his possessions in charity (dān) during Kumbha, leaving the festival with nothing of what he brought. Such accounts highlight the enduring significance and magnitude of Kumbha across history.

This chapter focuses on the historicity of Kumbha, exploring its development and cultural resilience through time.

7. **Kumbha: The Akhāḍās**

Chapter 7 explores the critical role of Akhāḍās in the Kumbha Melā, emphasising their spiritual, historical, and organisational importance. Akhāḍās, which combine ascetic training with martial practices, serve as guardians of Hindū Dharma and cultural heritage. Originating as wrestling arenas, they evolved into spiritual centres, particularly during times of external threats, such as Islamic invasions. Established by Śaṅkarācārya, the Daśnāmi Akhāḍās are classified into three categories: Śaiva, Vaiṣṇava, and Udāsīn, with newer Akhāḍās also emerging. The Akhāḍās play a central role in the Kumbha Melā by organising rituals, leading processions, and maintaining the spiritual essence of the event.

8. **Kumbha: Conclusion**
   The conclusion of Kumbha reflects on the enduring significance of the Kumbha Melā, which began as a divine gathering at the confluence of sacred rivers and evolved over centuries. It traces the Melā's historical development, from mythological roots to Ādi Śaṅkarācārya's role in organising it, and highlights the impact of colonialism on its structure. Despite modern challenges like commercialisation and environmental concerns, the Kumbha Melā remains a symbol of spiritual unity, purification, and devotion. It continues to inspire and connect people, embodying India's timeless spiritual heritage.

As we have traversed the various dimensions of Kumbha—mythological, Vaidik, Paurāṇik, philosophical, astrological, historical, geographical, and more—it becomes imperative to reflect on its future as a tradition deeply rooted in India's cultural and spiritual ethos.

Kumbha has long served as a reflection of India's wisdom, thought process, and spirituality—interwoven into a tradition that has evolved over centuries. From the time of ancient kings like Harṣa to the British era, the festival has gained the support of rulers, elites, and the masses, each contributing to its growth and cultural significance. Even today, the government supports its development through various initiatives, further cementing Kumbha's place in modern India.

Yet, as this ancient tradition continues to evolve, it faces a new challenge. The original, conventional Kumbha, a sacred and spiritual gathering, is now at a crossroads. With increasing government involvement and modern influences, a pressing concern arises: is the true essence of Kumbha still preserved, or is it at risk of being overshadowed by new, globalised norms?

While modernisation and technological advancements are inevitable, the question remains whether these changes will enhance or dilute the core spirit of Kumbha. The festival has always been a celebration of joy, knowledge, culture, and spirituality—values that should remain intact, even as the world witnesses Kumbha through the lenses of globalisation and digitalisation.

The role of technology should be to support, not overshadow, the spirit of Kumbha. It should serve to connect people and preserve the festival's heritage, rather than reducing it to a mere spectacle for global attention. Progress should not lead to destruction. The unfortunate reality of today's progress is that in the name of development, a path of destruction is being paved. Technology should help preserve Kumbha as the mythical, mystical event full of hidden meanings that it has always been, rather than distorting its essence in the pursuit of superficial progress.

As we move forward, we must ensure that Kumbha retains its identity as a festival rooted in Indian values and traditions and that it continues to be a beacon of unity, spirituality, and culture for generations to come. With this, I would like to conclude my words with the hope that this literature, a tribute to the Śrāut-Smārta Ṛṣi

Paraṁparā, can find its way into the hearts of the readers. And that it has served the purpose of being written. With This Hope, I hand over this book to the world of sophisticated readers who desire to read great literature. May my work be evaluated by them.

Mayur Pandey
George Town, Prayagraj—211002
Safalā Ekādaśī, Kṛṣṇa Pakṣa,
Pauṣa, Vikram Saṁvat 2081

Acknowledgments

With utmost sincerity and humility, I express my heartfelt gratitude to my parents, Dr. Shashank Pandey and Seema Pandey, who embody divine love and grace. Their unwavering support and guidance have shaped me into the person I am today, enabling me to undertake and complete this literary journey.

I revere Sītārām Ji—the Creator, Sustainer, Destroyer, Restrainer, and the ultimate Bestower of grace—whose divine inspiration has been the driving force behind this work.

I extend my gratitude to Prakṛti (Nature), the ultimate harmoniser, whose rhythm and beauty provided constant inspiration throughout this creative process.

My deepest respects and gratitude go to my Gurus and teachers, especially Pūjya Śaṅkarācārya Dvārikā Pīṭhādhiśvar Sadānanda Sarasvatī Jī Mahārāj, whose wisdom dispelled my doubts. I remain in awe of his humility and the warmth with which he welcomed me.

I sincerely acknowledge my sister, Anika Dubey, for her invaluable insights on the book's cover design, which serves as its first impression.

I also extend my gratitude to my brother, Kesari Nandan Pandey, for his unwavering support in various aspects of this book's completion.

My heartfelt appreciation goes to my elder brother, Manvendra Mishra, whose meticulous efforts in reviewing and refining the Sanskrit ślokas ensured their accuracy and authenticity.

I am also thankful to my dear friends, Gopal Verma and Heramb Mishra, for their thoughtful insights, which enriched the writing process.

To all those who have supported me on this journey —whether through guidance, encouragement, or inspiration—I remain forever indebted.

I also extend my sincere gratitude to the scholars, researchers, and institutions whose extensive work on Kumbha Melā and related subjects has laid a strong foundation for my own study. Their meticulous research, historical analyses, and spiritual insights have been invaluable in shaping my understanding and enriching this book. This work represents a modest contribution to the ever-expanding discourse on these profound traditions.

With deepest gratitude,

Mayur Pandey
George Town, Prayagraj—211002
Mokṣadā Ekādaśī, Śukla Pakṣa,
Mārgaśīrṣa, Vikram Saṁvat 2081

Transliteration

This book employs the IAST (International Alphabet of Sanskrit Transliteration) system, which was adopted at the Tenth International Congress of Orientalists held in Geneva on September 10, 1984. The system adopted the following notations to accurately represent the sounds of Sanskrit and other Indic languages in Roman script.

Image 1: IAST Transliteration Table[2]

On these principles the transliteration alphabet would be constituted thus—

a ā i ī u ū ṛ ṝ ḷ ḹ e ai o au

k kh g gh ṅ

c ch j jh ñ

ṭ ṭh ḍ ḍh ṇ

t th d dh n

p ph b bh m

y r l v ś ṣ s h ḻ ṁ m̐

visarga *ḥ*

jihvāmūlīya *ẖ*

upadhmānīya *ḫ*

As regards accents, the udātta would be represented by the acute ′

the svarita by the circumflex ^

the anudātta by the grave

[2] *Table from the Report of the Transliteration Committee, Pg 887, 1984, Tenth International Congress of the Orientalists.*

1. AN INTRODUCTION

In the āśrama of Maharṣi Bharadvāja at Prayāga, Maharṣi Yājñavalkya, along with many other saints, would visit every year during the month of Māgha, when the Sun entered the zodiac of Capricorn (Makara). They would perform their daily practices and take the holy dip at the Triveni Sangama. On one such visit, Maharṣi Yājñavalkya stayed a few days longer than the others. As he was preparing to leave, Sage Bharadvāja approached him with a request to answer some of his questions. These questions were all related to Lord Rāma. Bharadvāja asked, "Everyone says that Rāma is God and that one must chant the name of Rāma. But is this Rāma the same as the son of Daśaratha, or is he someone else?" Appreciating the curiosity of Sage Bharadvāja, Maharṣi Yājñavalkya decided to stay longer. He then explained everything about Rāma, addressing all the questions Bharadvāja had posed, and recited the complete Rāmcharitmānas to him.

This excerpt from Bālkāṇḍa in Rāmcharitmānas[3] emphasises the importance of taking a holy dip in the waters of Triveṇī at Prayāga during the auspicious time when the Sun enters the zodiac of Capricorn (Makara). This sacred period coincides with the Kumbha Melā, which is celebrated annually in Prayāga. However, the Kumbha Melā, a grander festival deeply rooted in Indian tradition, occurs only once every twelve years, in the same astrological configurations as Prayāga Kumbha.

Kumbha is more than just a festival or social congregation; it is a deeply rooted festival in Indian Culture. Now, in the era of technological advancements, when people have a wider scope for visiting Kumbha for prayers, worship, spiritual baths, and so on, things seem to be easier. However, in ancient times, when there was a lack of advanced technological support, people still managed to gather at the right place at the right time to celebrate the Festival with full enthusiasm. In 1942, Lord Linlithgow, the then Viceroy of India, was amazed when he saw such a large mass of people coming to Prayāgaraj at Prayāga Kumbha. He inquired of Mahāmana Madan Mohan Mālvīya about how so many people gathered here. He expected that there must be some announcement made or invitations sent. Mahāmana replied to the viceroy by showing him the Pañcāṅga (or the Indian Calendar based on Planetary positions) and said, "The whole country knows that when these planetary positions meet, the people know it is Kumbha, and they come to the city where Kumbha is supposed to be celebrated." It is particularly true for a Kumbha, as sending invitations or messages to lakhs and lakhs of people

---

[3] *The lines below are an exerpt of Rāmcaritamānas, Bālakaṇḍa Dohā 43 onwards.*

across the subcontinent thousands of years ago would have been an impractical approach to consider.

Additionally, the Saints who have lived in remote, secluded places for years come to Kumbha uninvitedly because they are aware of when Kumbha is traditionally held. It's all possible because of the accurate astronomical calculations presented by the Panchāṅg. Thus, Kumbha is a festival of inclusiveness, where people from all over the subcontinent come together without feeling superior or belonging to a particular caste.

Defining Kumbha:

कुम्भौ वैश्यापतो घटे।

द्विपाङ्के राक्षसे राशौ कुम्भं त्रिवृत्ति गुग्गुलौ॥

कुंभ्युखायां पाटलायां वारिपण्र्यां च कट्फले।

गर्भः कुक्षौ शिशौ संधौ भ्रूणे पनसकण्टके॥

(Anekartha Saṅgraha 2.310-311)

'Kumbha' is a sanskṛt term that means a 'pitcher' or 'earthen pot', as known to many people. Kumbha, as Kumbha Rāśī, indicates the name of the zodiac Aquarius when used in Jyotiṣa. Kumbha also refers to some more meanings, such as 'the two frontal muscles of an elephant', a husband of whore' and 'special yogic kṛyā'.

In Vaidik tradition, Kumbha was the name of 'the father of Sage Agastya', 'one of the three sons of Pralhād, the other two were Vīrochan and NiKumbha' and 'son of Kumbhakarna'.

In the Śramaṅ tradition, Kumbha was the name of the father of the nineteenth Jain Tīrthaṅkar,

Mallināth Ji, and also one of the 24 births of Gautama Buddha (Śākya Muni Gautama).

In history, the Rājpūta King, Mahārāṇā Kumbha, ruled the Kingdom of Mewar from 1433 to 1468.

According to the Śukranīti, Kumbha is a measure of weight and equals 2 droṇas, weighing around 24.576 kilograms.

In the Sthāpatya Ved, an upaveda of the Atharva Ved, Kumbha refers to a classification of a 'prāsādaṁ' temple or building as mentioned in Samarāṅgaṇasūtradhāra Chapter 63. In other instances, it is referred to as a 'capital'. It is sculptured as a part of a staṁbha (pillar).

In Āyurveda, Kumbha refers to various medicinal elements and plants. It signifies specific parts of the roots. It is also a term used for these floras— Prishnaparni (Uraria picta), Nutmeg (Myristica fragrans), the Pāṭalā tree (Stereospermum suaveolens), and Guggul (Commiphora wightii). Each of these plants has a unique role in traditional medicine, contributing to health and wellness through its therapeutic properties.

In Indian Classical Music, Kumbha is also a Rāginī. This Rāginī originated from the two prominent Rāgās—Saraswatī and Dhanashrī, Sangīt Dāmodara.

In special reference to this book and its main subject matter, Kumbha means a festival celebrated in 4 sacred cities during the special planetary combination of Jupiter (Bṛhaspati), Sun (Sūrya), and Moon (Candra), on the banks of holy rivers **'Gaṅgā in Haridwār'**, **'Gaṅgā, Yamunā, and**

Saraswatī in Prayāga', 'Godāvarī in Nāsik-Trayambakeśwar' and 'Siprā in Ujjayunī' which nourishes the nature with various yajñas, which results into cleansing of land and people away from sin, thus making the land and the people pious and virtuous and energised.

Kumbha: Etymology:

The word Kumbhaḥ originates from the Sanskṛta dhātu (root) 'kubhi', from the 'curādigaṇīya' group, which conveys the meaning "to cover" (kubhi ācchādane). It signifies completely covering or enclosing something, here with water and thus refers to a pot, pitcher, jar, or container for water. It also symbolically embodies the idea that brahman, as kāla (time), exists within the constituents of this universe (bhūta). The enlightened sages perceive brahman manifesting in diverse forms, yet they know that brahman remains unchanged and remains unattached to this samsāra, akin to 'vyom' (space) or ākāśa. This supreme reality, free from death and fear, is itself 'Kumbha'. The same idea is reflected in the Atharv Veda:

पूर्णः कुम्भोऽधि काल आहितस्तं वै पश्यामो बहुधा नु सन्तः ।
स इमा विश्वा भुवनानि प्रत्यङ्कालं तमाहुः परमे व्योमन् ॥

(Atharv Veda 19.53.3)

An alternative explanation of the word's construct arises from the combination of two terms, 'ku' and 'umbh', forming 'Kumbhaḥ', a masculine word in Sanskṛta vocabulary. The etymology is further elaborated in Śabdakalpadruma as follows:

- **Kum bhūmim umbhati jalena**: "That which fills the earth (ground) with water." By adding the suffix 'ac' to the root, the term acquires its complete form: 'Kumbhaḥ'.

The root 'umbh' belongs to the śakandhvāditvāt group of Sanskṛta roots. It denotes completeness (pūrṇatā), reflecting the pot's ability to hold and encompass water in its entirety.

In the Āpte Śabdakośa, the term is defined similarly as:

- **Kum bhūmim kutsitam vā umbhati pūrayati umbh-ac śakam:** This suggests that Kumbha can also refer to something that "fills the earth or something impure with water" — signifying its role in both purifying and containing.

Here are a few additional etymological constructs that help to provide various meanings of the term Kumbha :

	Etymology	Meaning / Interpretation
1	*Kam pṛthvīm bhāvayati poṣayati vividhayāgādibhiriti vā Kumbhaḥ*	Nourishes the earth through various sacrifices (yajñas).
2	*Kum pṛthvīm bhāpayati dīpayati tejo-vṛddhane-iti vā*	Illuminates the earth with brightness and enhances its radiance.
3	*Kuḥ pṛthvī ubhyate laṇḍūkrīyate pāpa-prakṣālanaiḥ puṇya-parivṛddhanaśca yena sah Kumbhaḥ*	Purifies the earth and elevates it with the removal of sin and growth of virtue.

4	*Kaṁ jalaṁ umbhati pūrayati avṛṣaṇādī-durbhikṣebhyo dūrayatī-iti Kumbhaḥ*	Fills and supplies water, especially during times of drought and famine.
5	*Kuṁ pṛthvīṁ umbhati pūrayati maṅgala-sammānādibhiriti Kumbhaḥ*	Fills the earth with auspiciousness, honor, and blessings.
6	*Kuṁ pṛthvīṁ bhāvayanti bhaviṣyat-kalyāṇādikāya mahatyākāśe sthitāḥ vṛhaspatyād-yoga-grahāḥ saṁyujya haridvār-prayāgādi tattat-puṇya-sthāna-viśeṣān-uddiśya*	That which signifies the welfare of the earth by alignment of celestial bodies, such as Jupiter others, in the great sky, particularly focusing or holy places like Prayāga and others, is referred t Kumbha.
7	*Kumbhayati amṛtena pūrayati sakala kṣut pipāsādi dwandjātaṁ nivartyati iti Kumbhaḥ*	That which fills with nectar (amṛta), satisfying all hunger and thirst and removing all dual afflictions (like hunger
8	*kutsitaṁ ubhbhayati dūrayati jagaddhitāyeti*	**It purifies, removes negativity, symbolises global welfare.**

This tabular presentation shows the range of meanings associated with the term Kumbha and its symbolic representations in various contexts.

Conclusion:

In his autobiography, Mahātmā Gāndhī reflects on his experience of the Kuṁbha Melā:

> "The day of the fair was now upon us. It proved to be a red-letter day for me. I had not gone to Hardvār with the sentiments of a pilgrim. I have never thought of frequenting places of pilgrimage in search of piety. But the seventeen lakh men that were reported to be there could not all be hypocrites or mere sightseers. I did not doubt that countless people among them had come to earn merit and for self-purification. It is difficult, if not impossible, to say to what extent this kind of faith uplifts the soul."

Gāndhī's words underscore the profound faith that draws millions to Kuṁbha, positioning it as more than a mere congregation. It is a spiritual movement deeply rooted in India's cultural ethos. Remarkably, this awe is not confined to Indian thinkers alone. Numerous esteemed scholars, both Indian and Western, who have visited or studied Kuṁbha, have expressed their admiration for its grandeur and the collective devotion it inspires. Among the Indian figures are Mahatma Gandhi, Pandit Jawaharlal Nehru, Swami Vivekananda, Dr S. Radhakrishnan, Dr K.K. Aziz, Mahamana Madan Mohan Malviya, Sri Aurobindo, Radhakrishnan Pillai, and Narendra Modi. The list of foreign scholars includes Sir John Woodroffe, David Frawley, Kama Maclean, Mark Twain, and Richard Lannoy.

2. Vaidik and Paurānik References

Finally, Yudhiṣṭhira decided to investigate the fate of his brothers. Upon reaching the lake where they had fallen, he was shocked to find his four valiant brothers lying lifeless. He suspected that the water was either enchanted or poisonous and blamed it for their demise. Resolving to share their fate, he approached the lake to drink. Suddenly, a Yakṣa appeared and declared, "This pond is mine. Your brothers perished because they drank from it without answering my questions. If you wish to live, you must answer them." Yudhiṣṭhira replied, "I do not seek to take what does not belong to me unjustly. I will answer your questions with honesty and respect." Among the many profound questions posed by the Yakṣa, one held particular significance to the philosophy and essence of Kumbha:

Yakṣa: *What is truly amazing in this world?*

Yudhiṣṭhira: *The most amazing thing is that, though humans are mortal, everyone lives as if they will be here forever.*

This excerpt from the Mahābhārata, specifically from Van Parva, clearly shows that everyone experiences different life events, has different desires, and performs various actions. In short, two identical twins are also of two distinct natures. The amazing part comes with the fact that all beings have five fundamental similarities in themselves: (i) the desire for eternal life, (ii) being free from ignorance and identical with consciousness, (iii) being immersed in bliss or 'ananda', (meaning everyone wishes to do away with the sufferings of all three kinds, daihik, daivik, and bhautik meaning bodily, divine, and materialistic, respectively), (iv) being independent and (v) controller of all things. Every person has these fundamental desires, and we come to a rational conclusion that when the qualities of two substances match absolutely, it is by no mistake that the two different things are the same 'tatva' (element). Thus, we get one tattva as the basis of all beings, known as 'ātmā' in Sanatan dharma. So, ātmā or ātma-tatva is the ultimate source of energy, embodying eternal life, pure consciousness, and bliss. People who are suffering in this world are trapped in the vicious cycle of birth and death. Getting free from this cycle and realising our true nature is 'mokṣa' or 'mukti'. Thus, Kumbha as a festival is a congregation where the core idea is to help people overcome their sufferings and attain the nectar of life, for which Kumbha is used as a symbol in the Vedas, Purāṇas, and all Indian traditions.

Indian scholars and philosophies have paved paths for laymen to attain mukti in the most plausible ways. The Vedas state, 'ekam evādvitīyam brahma sadasadrūpam sadasadasītam,' which means that everything we perceive is Brahma. For further clarification, they add, "etaj-jñeyaṁ nityam evātmasaṁstham nātaḥ param veditavyaṁ hi kiñcit; bhoktā bhogyaṁ preritāraṁ ca matvā sarvaṁ proktaṁ trividhaṁ brahmam etat," indicating that this world has three aspects of Brahma— being bhokta, bhogya and preritaram (the enjoyer, the enjoyed and the power which brings enjoyment). The first is Jeeva, the second is Prakṛti or Māyā, which is the aparā śakti of Brahma, and the third is Brahma itself, in his true form. However, in reality, the Vedas view existence as one, and that He, the supreme, is only manifested in all forms. Scholars seek Him in every form—ekaṁ sat bahudhā viprā vadanti. They say that Viṣṇu was in his deep sleep in kṣīr sāgar when he thought of creation— so'kāmayata bahu syāṁ prajāyeyeti. So, from him, all forms and creations manifested.

However, the Vedas also argue that, as Brahma is one and absolute, the path to reach Him is also one —nānyaḥ panthā vidyate'yanāya. This knowledge that leads to the truth is known as Brahmavidyā or Ātmavidyā and is considered the highest form of knowledge. After learning this, nothing remains unknown. The quest for everything ends here.

Thus, the path to reach God is one, and the three paths told by the Vedas and Gītā—karma yoga, bhakti yoga, and jñāna yoga- are three continuous chapters of the same path.

This philosophical theory is discussed here because it appears in the Vedas, which also mentions the term Kumbha numerous times.

Kumbha: Reference in Vedas:

Sometimes, it refers to a kalaśa (pot) used in pūjā or karma kāṇḍa, in a philosophical context, relating it to life. At other times, it mentions the festival Kumbha without explicitly using the term Kumbha.

Let us first have a look at the Ślokas where the term is used along with its references:

जघान॑ वृ॒त्रं स्वधि॑ति॒र्वनेव रु॒रोज॒ पुरो॒ अर॑द॒न्न सिन्धू॑न् ।
बि॒भेद॑ गि॒रिं नव॒मिन्न कु॒म्भमा गा इन्द्रो॑ अकृणुत स्व॒युग्भि॑: ॥

(Ṛg Saṁhitā 10.89.7)

"(Indra) slew Vṛtra as an axe (cuts down) a tree; he demolished the cities (of the foes), he dug out the rivers; he shattered the cloud like a new pitcher; with his allies (the Maruts) he recovered the cattle."

Here, a fierce form of Indra is portrayed. He is the deity most frequently mentioned in the Ṛg Veda. Indra is depicted as the one who brings an end to the forces of obstruction, represented by Vṛtra. This obstruction blocks the flow of rivers and the prosperity of the people. The analogy of shattering a cloud like a new pitcher emphasises his role as a bringer of rain, abundance, and wealth.

Another set of references brings a different aspect related to Indra, Kumbha, and the nectar of life, soma or amṛta. The Atharva Veda mentions Kumbha as a kalaśa, or pot, filled with various things. These are all symbols of prosperity, and they are even related to Amṛta, or nectar of life, which is made from kshīr, or milk itself.

एमां प॑रि॒स्रुत॑ः कु॒म्भ आ द॑ध्नः क॒लशैँरगुः ॥

(Atharv Veda 3.12.7)

"Bring this pot, filled with curd and honey, that has been overflowing, moving with the pitchers into this shālā."

This highlights the significance of kalaśa from Vedic times to the present day, as it is placed in every Vaidik ritual, including Kumbha or Kalaśa. Additionally, milk and honey are symbols of prosperity in agrarian societies. Adding to this, as we delve deeper into processing milk, it will give— Doodh (Milk) → Malai (Cream) → Dahi (Curd) → Makhan (Butter) → Ghṛta (Ghī) → Māṇḍa.

ततस्तस्य समुद्रस्य तज्जातमुदकम पयः ।

रसोत्तमैर्विमिश्रं से तत् क्षीरादभूद् घृतम॥

(Mahābhārata 1.5.18.28)[4]

The texts even describe a technique for further processing Māṇḍa, which, if followed through many steps, will result in the formation of amṛta or nectar. Thus, with this reference added, Kumbha, mentioned in the Atharva Veda and overflowing with honey and milk, is also related to the basic idea of Kumbha, i.e., to attain eternal life.

At an another instance the term is used for prosperity as said before. Lets have a look on it also:

कोशं॑ दुहन्तिक॒लशं॑ चतु॒र्बिल॒मिडां॑ धे॒नुं मधु॑मतीं स्व॒स्तये॑।

ऊर्जं॑ मद॒न्तीमदि॑ति॒जने॑ष्व॒ग्ने॒ मा हिं॑सीः प॒रमे व्यो॑मन् ॥

(Atharva Veda 18.4.30)

---

[4] *Refer the Mahābhārata published by Gītā Press Gorakhpur, Volume 1*

"The Vaidik speech is a cow that provides the milk of knowledge for us. This refers to the Vaidik speech, which makes our lives exceedingly sweet. This cow of Vaidik speech— for welfare — is being milked. This Vaidik speech cow is a repository of knowledge. A pot that contains all the arts, and— this Vaidik vessel has four udders representing the four Vedas: Ṛg, Yajur, Sāma, and Atharva. From these four teats, the milk of knowledge flows."

कुम्भो वनिष्छुर्जनिता शचीभिर्यस्मिन्नग्रे योन्यां गर्भोंऽअन्तः।
प्लाशिर्व्यक्तः शतधारऽउत्सों दुहे न कुम्भी स्वधां पितृभ्यः ॥८७॥
(Yajur Veda 19.87)

In the Yajur Veda, the womb is referred to as Kumbha, symbolising a sacred vessel that protects and nurtures the developing child. It emphasises the importance of parents safeguarding the child, highlighting the sanctity of life and creation.

युवं नरा स्तुवते पन्त्रियायं कुक्षीवंते अरदतं पुरंधिम्।
कारोतराच्छफादश्वस्य वृष्णः शतं कुम्भाँ असिञ्चतं सुरायाः॥
(Ṛg Veda 1.116.7)

The Ṛg Veda mentions Kumbha as a pot, but these verses connect to the philosophical essence of the Kumbha festival. In this context, the Aśvinī Kumāras are praised for safeguarding the city of Kakṣīvān and establishing a hundred Kumbhas within it, purifying them with water from a vessel shaped like a horse's hoof.

यः सोमः कुलशेष्याँ अन्तः पवित्र आहितः। तमिन्दुः परि षस्वजे॥

(Ṛg Veda 9.12.5)
(Sām Veda, Uttarārchik 9.3.5)

This verse is mentioned in both places, and it means, "The water must touch the Soma that is kept in Kalaśa."

In the same narrative, flowing another Ṛg Vaidik verse adds up to the theory:

आपूर्णो अस्य कुलशः स्वाहा सेक्तेव कोशं सिसिचे पिबंध्यै।
समुं प्रिया आवंवृत्रन्मदाय प्रदक्षिणिदभि सोमांसु इन्द्रम्॥
(Ṛg Veda 3.32.15)

The hymn means simply that "The kalaśas filled with soma are kept for Indra to drink".

Furthermore, another verse conveys this meaning:

दिव्यः सुपुर्णोंऽव चक्षि सोमु पिन्वन्धाराः कर्मणा देववींतौ।
एन्दौ विश कुलशं सोमुधानुं क्रन्दन्निहि सूर्यस्योप रश्मिम्॥
(Ṛg Veda 9.97.33)

This means that Indra has entered into the Kumbhas (pots) filled with soma.

Thus, the soma is the amṛta or nectar, and it is kept for Indra, who is the king of all the gods. The śāstras mention a peculiar fact in one of their hymns:

यथा सुराणाम् अमृतं प्रवीलां जलं स्वधा।
सुधा यथा च नागानां तथा गङ्गाजलं नृणाम्॥

"As amṛta is for gods, Swadhā jal is for pitaras (ancestors), Sudhā is with Nāgas, in the same way, Gaṅgājal is to humans."

As we see these uses of the Kumbha term "kubha" in the Vedas, we now know that all these terms were used to symbolise a pot or pitcher representing prosperity, wealth, and happiness. In a special context, Kumbha contained milk or soma, which is associated with amṛta, or nectar.

Kumbha: Reference in Purāṇas:

The Purāṇas extensively discuss the Kumbha festival and the spiritual benefits of visiting sacred places such as Haridwar, Prayāg, Nāsik, and Ujjainī. While detailing the festival's timing and locations, they often refrain from explicitly using the term 'Kumbha', likely due to the Indian tradition of maintaining secrecy around mantras and auspicious timings. Nevertheless, the festival continues to be celebrated grandly every 12 years at these four holy sites.

The Idea Of Kumbha at Four Sites:

The mention of four Kumbhas is made in the Atharva Veda, in the śloka: **'चतुरः कुम्भाः…'**, but it refers to the Kumbhas in a deep philosophical sense related to the attainment of Dharma, Artha, Kāma, and Mokṣa.

चतुरः कुम्भांश्चतुर्धा ददामि क्षीरेण पूर्णाँ उदकेन दध्ना।
एतास्त्वा धाराा उप यन्तु सर्वाः स्वर्गे लोके मधुमत्पिन्वमाना उप त्वा
तिष्ठन्तु पुष्करिणीः समन्ताः ॥
(Atharva Veda 4.34.7)

However, in the Agni Purāṇa, a more elaborate version of Chatuṣ Kumbha is mentioned. The chapter of Kalaśādhivāsana mentions that these pitchers should be consecrated in the four quarters with water-filled pitchers for consecration. The pitchers should be placed with due regard for consecration.

स्नानकुम्भेषु कुम्भास्ताश्चतुर्दिक्षवधिवासयेत्।
कलशा स्थापनीयास्तु अभिषेकार्थमादरात्॥
(Agni Purāṇa 57.8)

The Agni Purāṇa then prescribes chanting this mantra and performing the karmakāṇḍa:

स्योना। पृथिवि। नः। भव। अनृक्षरा। निवेशनीतिं निऽवेशनी ॥
यच्छं। नः। शर्म। सप्रथा इतिं सऽप्रथाः॥
(Yajur Veda 36.13)

Additionally, the mention of auspicious planetary locations is scattered across various Purāṇas, which describe the rituals to be performed at these places and the benefits one can gain. Below are the references from the verses of the Purāṇas, starting with mentions of Haridwār, followed by Prayāga, Nāsik, and Ujjayunī.

Haridwār:

The Purāṇas highlight Haridwār's significance, stating that although there are thousands of tīrthas, one who bathes during the saṅkrānti of Kumbha and Meṣa Rāśī attains greatness akin to that of Bṛhaspati and Sūrya:

अन्यानि वै महाभागे सन्ति तत्र सहस्रशः।
योऽस्मिन्क्षेत्रे नरः सनायात्कुम्भगेज्येऽजगे रवौ॥
(Bṛhannāradīya Purāṇa 2.66.44)

In the same continuation, Prayāga and other tīrthas, including Haridwār, are mentioned for their millions of times more puṇya during Amāvāsyā, Saṅkrānti, and especially during Varuṇa Yoga, Mahā Varuṇa Yoga, and Mahā Mahā Varuṇa Yoga.

स तु स्याद्वाक्पतिः साक्षात्प्रभाकर इवापरः।

अथ याते प्रयागादिपुण्यतीर्थे पृथूदके॥ ४५॥

अथ यो वारुणे योगे महावारुणके तथा।

महामहावारुणे च स्नायात्तत्र विधानतः॥ ४६॥

सम्पूज्य ब्राह्मणान् भक्त्या स लभेद्ब्रह्मणः पदम्।

संक्रान्तौ वाप्यमायां वा व्यतीपाते युगादिके॥ ४७॥

पुण्येऽहनि तथान्यद्दै यत्किंचिद्दानमाचरेत्।

तत्तु कोटिगुणं भूयात्सत्यमेतन्मयोदितम्॥ ४८॥

गङ्गाद्वारं स्मरेद्यो वै दूरसंस्थोऽपि मानवः।

सद्गतिं स समाप्नोति स्मरन्नन्ते यथा हरिम्॥ ४९॥

यं यं देवं हरिद्वारे पूजयेत्प्रयतो नरः।

स स देवः सुप्रसन्नः पूर्येत्तन्मनोरथान्॥ ५०॥

(Bṛhannāradīya Purāṇa 2.66.45-48)

Such a person achieves unparalleled wisdom. They gain immense merit by visiting holy places like Prayāga or Pṛthūdaka. Bathing during the Varuṇa Yoga, Mahā Varuṇa Yoga, or even the Mahā Mahā Varuṇa Yoga, following proper rituals, leads to the highest spiritual attainment. Worshipping Brāhmaṇas with devotion during such auspicious times grants the supreme state of Brahman.

On sacred days like Saṅkrānti, Vyatipāta, or the beginnings of a Yuga, any charitable act multiplies its merit a million times—this is the eternal truth. Even thinking of Gaṅgādvāra (Haridwār) from afar grants liberation, just like remembering Lord Hari at the time of death. Whatever deity one worships with devotion at Haridwār, that deity becomes pleased and fulfils all their desires.

Thus, although the name of the festival Kumbha is not mentioned, the planetary combinations are still accurate here and up to the mark. In all other references to the Kumbha, the same pattern is followed. The astronomical combinations, along with their associated rituals and benefits, are mentioned without directly naming the festival.

Prayāga:

After Haridwār, Prayāga Kumbha takes place in a cyclic order. In the Bṛhannāradīya Purāṇa, the complete 63rd chapter is dedicated to the glory of taking a holy bath in Prayāga at the time when the Sūrya and Candra are in Makara Rāśī and Bṛhaspati is:

पृथिव्यां यानि तीर्थानि पुर्यः पुण्यास्तथा सति।

स्नातुमायान्ति ता वेण्यां माघे मकर भास्करे॥

(Bṛhannāradīya Purāṇa 12.63.7)

"All the holy places on Earth, which are immensely pious, come to bathe in the river confluence during the Magha month when the Sūrya (Sun) enters Kumbha (Capricorn)."

स्नात्वा हि ये माकर भास्करोदये तीर्थे प्रयागे सुरसिन्धुसंगमे।

तेषां गृहद्द्वारमंगलकरोति भृंगावली कुञ्जरकर्णतडीता॥

(Bṛhannāradīya Purāṇa 2.63.40)

"Those who bathe during the time of Makara Saṅkrānti at the confluence of the Gaṅgā and Yamunā at Prayāga, their homes are blessed with auspiciousness, just like the hum of bees and the sounds of elephants' ears."
The elephants here are said to be at the door of the

person who takes a bath. Elephants symbolise prosperity and wealth, and the movement of their ears constantly moves the bees.

अमृतं भद्रे कथ्यते भद्रे सा वेणी भुवि संगता।
यस्यां माघे मुहूर्तं तु देवनामपि दुर्लभम्॥

(Bṛhannāradīya Purāṇa 2.63.6)

The sacred river confluence of Gaṅgā and Yamunā is said to be amṛta on Earth (Amṛta) and is highly auspicious. Bathing in it during the Magha month for even a moment is said to be rare, even for the gods.

In the case of Prayāga Kumbha, the most notable aspect is that this festival occurs every 12 years in this city. However, every year in Mārgaśīrṣa, people from all over the subcontinent come to undertake Kalpavāsa, i.e., a special one-month stay during which they accumulate puṇya equivalent to the puṇya they could have earned by performing those practices for one kalpa (the time equivalent to one day and one night of Brahmā). Thus, while the Kumbha occurs every 12 years, the city celebrates the Māgha Mela annually with the same ethos. This makes Prayāga a sacred hub of spiritual activities. The city is always ready to welcome guests with warm hospitality. In the Sangam Kṣetra of Prayāgarāja, people perform Kalpavāsa and gain immense spiritual benefits.

Nāsik:

In the case of Nāsik, located on the bank of the Godāvarī, the Purāṇas extensively describe the rituals and the benefits gained from performing them, including attaining the eternal abode of Śiva.

20

The astrological combinations state that when Bṛhaspati enters Siṃha Rāśi, the Godāvarī, also called Gautamī, becomes tribhuvanapāvanī—one who purifies all three worlds. At this special time, all tīrthas come to her, as declared by Śiva Himself to Pārvatī:

त्वं गौतमी सदा पूज्या सर्वेषामपि मुक्तिदा।

विशेषतस्तु सिंहस्ते मयि त्रैलोक्ये पावनी॥

यानि कानि च तीर्थानि स्वर्गमृत्युरसतले।

त्वां स्नातु तानि यास्यन्ति मयि सिंहस्थितेऽम्बिके॥

(Brahma Purāṇa 152.38–39)

"There are three and a half crore (koṭi) pilgrimage sites in the three worlds. All these converge in the Gautamī when Guru (Bṛhaspati) enters Siṃha. Bathing in the Gautamī during this period is equivalent to sixty thousand years of virtue. A single bath in the Godāvarī, when Vṛhaspati is in Siṃha, yields the same merit."

तिस्रः कोटयोऽर्धकोटि च तीर्थानि भुवनत्रये।

तानि स्नातु समायान्ति गङ्गायां सिंहगे गुरौ॥

षष्टिवर्षसहस्राणि भागीरथ्यावगाहनाम्।

सकृद्गोदावरी स्नानं सिंहयुक्ते वृहस्पतौ॥

(Brahma Purāṇa 175.83–84)

The ślokas mentioned above refer to both Godāvarī and Gautamī, which are names for the same river. As the river was brought to South India by Ṛṣi Gautama, it is called Gautamī in his honour. It is also known as Dakṣiṇa Gaṅgā because its origin is similar to that of the Gaṅgā, and its location is south of the Vindhya mountain range.

गोदावर्यां सिंहमासे स्नायात् सिंह वृहस्पतौ।
शिवलोकप्रदमिति शिवेनोक्त तथा पूरा॥
(Śiva Purāṇa 1.12.22–23)

Śiva Himself mentions in the Śiva Purāṇa:
"The bath in the Godāvarī during the month of Siṃha, when Guru is also in Siṃha, bestows Śiva's abode."

सिंहस्थे च गुरौ तत्र यो गच्छति समाहित।
स्नत्वा च विधिना तत्र पितृस्तर्पयेत तथा॥
स्वर्ग गच्छन्ति पितरो निरये पतिता अपि।
स्वर्गस्तथा पितरस्तस्य मुक्तिभाजो न संशयः॥
(Varāha Purāṇa 1.71.47–48)

"If, when Bṛhaspati is in Siṃha, one bathes there and propitiates the ancestors as per prescribed rituals, even those who have fallen into hell will ascend to heaven, and those already in heaven will attain liberation."

These ślokas highlight the sanctity of the Godāvarī, with Śiva Himself proclaiming that those who bathe in the Godāvarī at the designated time will achieve liberation. Likewise, bathing in the Śiprā River during such auspicious astronomical conditions guarantees the devotee's arrival in Śiva's abode.

Ujjayunī:

The Skanda Purāṇa, in Avantikā Khaṇḍa, Avantikā Māhātmya, highlights a special astrological combination for visiting Ujjayunī, taking baths, giving donations (dāna), and performing rituals. Chapter 50 of the Skanda Purāṇa glorifies the Śiprā River with great reverence and wonder:

माधवे मासि संप्राप्ते निमज्जंति नरोत्तमाः।
न तेषां निरयं किंचिच्छिवरुपाश्रंति ते॥
(Skanda Purāṇa 5.1.50.40)

"If excellent men take a bath in it during the month of Mādhava, they do not fall into hell at all. They move about in the form of Śiva."

अवन्तीयात्रा कर्तव्या प्रयत्नेन मुमुच्चुणा।
माधवेऽपि विशेषेण ह्यवन्तीस्नानमाचतत्।
यो हि वैशाखमासाद्य अवन्त्यां व्यास ! मानवः॥
सवत्सरव्रती स्नातस्तीर्थे यथाविधि।
दत्त्वा दानानि सर्वाणि समूल फलमश्नुते॥
(Skanda Purāṇa 5.1.82.15-17)

The Skanda Purāṇa thus emphasises bathing in the Śiprā during the month of Mādhava. In the Indian calendar, the month of Mādhava corresponds to Vaiśākha, which is still celebrated today as the time of the Kumbha Melā.

Conclusion:

Kumbha is mentioned in the Vedas as used for a pot overflowing with milk and honey, while it symbolises wealth and prosperity many times. It is worth noting that the idea of catur-Kumbha was given in the Atharva Veda, as described above. Still, by the time of Agni Purāṇa, it had grown more deeply, and even the mention of astrological combinations has been found in various Purāṇas. The Kumbha at Prayāga is a special case for two reasons. Firstly, Kumbha in Prayāga occurs at intervals of 12 years, but the Māgha Melā is celebrated annually. Secondly, it is the tīrtharāja, situated at the confluence of three rivers: the Gaṅgā, the Yamunā, and the Sarasvatī. In the cases of Haridwar and Prayagraj, the Ardha Kumbha is also celebrated every six years. This tradition is not the same in the case of Nāsika or Ujjayunī. The Purāṇas even mention the acts that need to be performed in special combinations at certain places. Examples include bathing in holy rivers, giving alms, practising dhyāna (meditation), and others. The Purāṇas glorify rivers greatly and mention their benefits with considerable assurance. Remarkably, this age-old tradition has persisted through time. Even in today's advanced era, people across the nation and around the world honour their ancestral culture, making the Kumbha Melā a global attraction.

3. The Story as in Purāṇas

*The author of **"I Found No Peace**," Mr Weg Miller, states that even eyewitness accounts cannot always be trusted to be accurate. Two individuals perceive the same event differently, and each person's imagination operates uniquely. Even in letters and official documents, meanings are often altered. Given this, how can the description of historical events from thousands of years ago be considered entirely true?*

*In reality, this is why the authors of ārṣa itihāsa, such as Vālmīki and Vyāsa, the sages behind the Rāmāyaṇa and the Mahābhārata, did not rely on **pratyakṣa (direct perception), anumāna (inference), saṁvāda-dātāḥ (informants)**, written records, or letters. Instead, they composed history based on **samādhi-janita ṛtambharā prajñā**—a state of consciousness that reveals absolute truth.*

This excerpt is taken from the book Rāmrājya and Marxvāda, written by Swāmī Hariharānanda Sarasvatī Śrī Karpātrī Jī in 1959. It seems correct that any human narrative will have a biased approach, and a human interpretation will always be involved. Before that time, history and mythology were not distinct entities. During the Renaissance, European philosophers adopted a new perspective on the study of history. A new approach involved the cause-and-effect system that is always present. Anything that didn't fit in that approach was declared to be a mythology, thus excluding it from the scope of history. Although it narrowed the scope of history, it introduced a scientific temperament to the field. This was of great benefit to the historiography. In the Indian context, there is a different tradition known as the Purāṇa. It was a tradition that wrote a history of events, including an ethical approach to it. It inculcated dilatative principles, dogmas, and lectures to help people understand. Although it had narratives of supernatural existence and events, it could not all be taken as gossip. It had an essence in itself.

प्राग्वृत्तकथनं चैकराजकृत्यमिषादितः।
यस्मिन् स इतिहासः स्यात् पुरावृत्तः स एव हि॥
(Śukra Nīti 4.293)

"Itihāsa is that which narrates past events in the context of describing royal duties, religious conduct, and other significant matters. That which deals with ancient occurrences is indeed itihāsa."

Historians, such as Frederick Eden Pargiter, an orientalist, have established many facts based on their scientific research. Firstly, the Purāṇas have a rich history in India and the world. Secondly, they have demonstrated the scientific method for

extracting historical information from the Purāṇas. They were successful at removing the dynasties and lineages of Kaliyuga. Thirdly, they have proven that the Purāṇas are more than just a source of history; rather, they are a
way of historiography, the traditional way of historiography, thus making it an 'epic history'. Scholars like Bimal Churn Law have even used the Purāṇas to extract the ancient names of places and use them to learn the geography of Ancient India. In his book Historical Geography of Ancient India, he says, "The Epics and Purāṇas are recognised as a rich
mine of geographical knowledge about ancient India."

The Purāṇas have ten characteristic features, being (i) sarga (refers to the creation of the universe), (ii) visarga (to sub-creation), (iii) sthānam (to the planetary systems), (iv) poṣaṇam (to protection), (v) ūtayaḥ (to the creative impetus), (vi) manvantara (to the changes of Manus), (vii) īśa-anukathāḥ (to the science of God), (viii) nirodhaḥ (to returning to the divine abode), (ix) muktiḥ (to liberation), and (x) āśrayaḥ (to the ultimate refuge or summum bonum). This is given concerning the śloka below:

अत्र सर्गो विसर्गश्च स्थानं पोषणमूतयः।

मन्वन्तरेशानुकथा निरोधो मुक्तिराश्रयः॥

(Śrīmad Bhāgavat Purāṇa 2.10.1)

Many aspects of Indian historiography fall outside the scope of modern historiography. However, it does come with the effect that the contemporary apparatus of cause and causation can still gain a lot from references in the Purāṇas. Thus, any piece of information available in either Purāṇas or any other scriptural text must not be discarded just because it is a piece of mythology. We must find a way to extract the information from those pieces. Now, it is evident in the context of Kuṁbha also. As the Purāṇas are the epic history of Indian culture, we must look to them as a source of information. This will not only help us gain special insights into the reasons why it started, but also provide a way for us to explore Indian history from the perspective of our ancestors.

In the cultural context, we find a basis for the celebration of Kuṁbha:

- The Paurāṇik stories of Samudra Manthana, Amṛta Kalaśa Sthāpan by Garuḍa in Śrī Bhāgavata Purāṇa.

- The planetary combinations are based on the Jyotiṣa Śāstra.

- The Adhidaiva forms play the characters in the story, such as Bṛhaspati, Sūrya, Candramā, Rāhu, Ketu, etc.

This section explores stories mentioned in the Purāṇas that are said to be the reason for the celebration of Kuṁbha. The next chapters will discuss in detail the astronomical and astrological aspects of Kuṁbha, as well as its philosophical aspects.

There are two overarching stories, with some changes in the Rāmāyaṇa, Mahābhārata, and Purāṇas. Both stories are claimed to be true in the case of the Kuṁbha due to the effect of Kalpa-bheda, with some changes in every text. Rather, it is a single two-fold story. The first is the Samudra Manthana story, and the second one is the conflict between Vinatā, mother of Aruṇa and Garuḍa, and Kadrū, mother of Nāgas. We shall now examine the story, taking into account the stage settings with minor adjustments, starting with the Mahābhārata, the largest epic ever written, and then the Harivaṁśa Purāṇa. Then, we will examine the Brahma Purana, Viṣṇu Purana, and Skanda Purana. Finally, we will have a glance at Śrīmad Bhāgavata Purāṇa.

Mahābhārata:

The Mahābhārata is published in six heavy volumes by Gītā Press, Gorakhpur, at an affordable price. In the Āstīka Parva, mentioned in the Ādi Parva of the Mahābhārata, two stories are mentioned, both related to the Kuṁbha. The first story goes as follows—

"Once upon a time, the devatās met at Mount Meru to discuss the ways of getting the Amṛta. Bhagavān Nārāyaṇa told them to do Samudra Manthana, or churning of the ocean, and then get the rare things, including the nectar. The devatās needed support from the Asuras, so they went and convinced them. Then they both reached Mount Mandarāñcala, and with the help of Anantaśeṣa, they brought him as the churner of the sea. Furthermore, they obtained consent from the Sāgara, who also requested his share in Amṛta. After agreeing to his terms, they asked for Bhagavān Kacchapa, who was located at the bottommost part of the Samudra, to serve as the base for Mandarāñcala. The process started, and Nāga Vāsuki was chosen to be the rope for churning the Mandarāñcala. Thus, everyone contributed their share, and Devarāja Indra pressed the Mandarāñcala with his Vajra to maintain the balance. The devatās were at the tail side, while the asuras were at the head side of Vāsuki.

After some time, the millions of species living in the Samudra got grounded in the sea, while those living in the mountain started to fall into the sea and experienced the same fate. Vāsuki was uncomfortable with being used as a rope, and thus, he began to spit out flames and venom into the atmosphere. The clouds began to rain, protecting the devatās, while the trees at the top caught fire due to the continuous rubbing against each other. The mountain caught a huge forest fire, and Indra used his powers to summon the clouds and make heavy rain to put out that fire. Then the herbs and latex from trees with special medicinal properties fell into the sea, and the water turned into milk. The milk churned up was now turned into ghṛta (ghī). (The same process was described in the previous chapter of this narrative of the Mahābhārata.)

The devatās were then tired, and so were the asuras; they went to Brahmā and Viṣṇu and told them about the same. At the request of Brahmā, Viṣṇu blessed them with power, and everyone started churning again. Then, the special things began to come, of which the coming of Dhanvantari with a white-coloured Kumbha or Kalaśa filled with nectar was the most important. Then, after further harsh churning, the Kālakūṭa poison came out, and everyone started dying because of it. Śiva drank it and stopped it in his neck; thus, he was named Nīlakaṇṭha. Furthermore, the nectar was taken by the asuras by use of power, and Viṣṇu took the Mohinī avatāra to get the Amṛta back. Mohinī made the asuras sit in a line, but she was reluctant to give the nectar to the asuras, and only the devatās benefited from the nectar of life through her.

Rāhu understood that Mohinī had misogyny against him. He sat in the row of devatās. As Rāhu drank Amṛta successfully, he was beheaded by the time the Amṛta reached his neck. Since Sūrya and Candramā were the ones who revealed his secret to Viṣṇu, their rivalry deepened further[5]. After giving Amṛta to all the devatās, Viṣṇu left his Mohinī form. Later, in the Devasura Saṅgrāma, or the war between the devatās and the asuras, Viṣṇu appeared in two forms: Nara and Nārāyaṇa. The devatās gave the nectar to Bhagavān Nara to keep it safe.

The other part of the story, which continues after this in the same Āstīka Parva, describes the two wives of Prajāpati Kaśyapa, named Vinatā and Kadrū. Vinatā was the mother of Aruṇa and Garuḍa, while Kadrū was the mother of serpents. Once, they made a bet on the colour of the tail of the Ucchaiśravā horse, a mythical and beautiful horse that emerged from the ratnas, or jewels, of the Samudra Manthana. The terms of their bet were that the one who lost would be the slave of the winner. Vinatā claimed the tail to be white, while Kadrū affirmed it to be black.

They both went to the horse, crossing the unfathomable sea, as described in the Mahābhārata. The part further reveals that Kadrū ordered her black-coloured serpents to cover the tail of the horse so that she could win. When they both reached, they

---

[5] *The mythological explanation for Sūrya Grahaṇa and Candra Grahaṇa connects to the story of Rāhu and Ketu in the Purāṇas. Meanwhile, Āryabhaṭa, in his Āryabhaṭīya (499 CE), provided a scientific explanation, identifying eclipses as the Earth's shadow on the Moon or the Moon obstructing the Sun's light, aligning with modern astronomical understanding.*

had a glimpse of the horse from a distance. The tail being black, as perceived by both, made Vinatā a slave to Kadrū. Had they gone a little closer to the horse, it would have been a completely different history. However, as there are no accidents in the universe's events, but only planned incidents, the story unfolds into darker chapters. Kadrū made Vinatā her servant, and years later, her son Garuḍa, born as a result of the Vālakhilyas' yajñas, wanted to free his mother, along with her wife, from Kadrū's slavery.

He asked the nāgas or serpents about a way to get rid of this slavery. They asked for Amṛta in return. Garuḍa accepted and went to the Svarga Loka, where the devatās were specially protecting the Amṛta. They knew that Garuḍa was coming, as informed by Bṛhaspati to Indra. Garuḍa saw the Kalaśa and defeated the entire army of devatās alone. Later, he fought with Indra, and although he surrendered one of his wings out of respect for Indra, he still managed to take away the Amṛta for his nāga brothers.

Garuḍa kept the Amṛta on the kuśa āsana, and the nāgas went to take a bath. Meanwhile, Indra came and took away the nectar of life, which belonged to the devatās. Thus, as Garuḍa brought and gave the Amṛta to the nāgas, he was able to free his mother and wife from the slavery of Kadrū.

Harivaṁśa Purāṇa:

Harivaṁśa Purāṇa is the 'khila bhāg' of the Mahābhārata, which can also be said to be the appendix of the Mahābhārata. It elaborates on the stories mentioned briefly in the Mahābhārata, particularly the life of Śrī Kṛṣṇa, his genealogy, pastimes, and the historical context of his life.

In the thirtieth chapter of Harivaṁśa Purāṇa, the narrative unfolds as follows:

"The devatās, along with asuras, came to the seaside and decided to put some medicinal herbs into the sea before churning. They agreed to collaborate to get nectar, with mutual benefits. The devatās and asuras both wanted the amṛta; by obtaining it, they would become shape-shifters. Then they churned for one thousand years. The Mount Mandarāñcala was the churner; Nāg Vāsuki was the rope, and the Kacchapāvatāra was made the base of Mount Mandarāñcala.

Then, when they put the herbs in the sea and churned for a thousand years, the salty water of the sea changed into milk and then into amṛta. From the Samudra Manthana, they gained items, which include Dhanvantari, Madya, Lakṣmī, Kaustubha Maṇi, and Candramā. They were followed by the horse Ucchaiśravā. Then the amṛta came out. The amṛta was stored in a Kumbha, which the asuras stole. The devatās claimed the amṛta, and then they fought with the asuras. Sūrya and Candramā exposed Rāhu, and Viṣṇu beheaded him. Then ṛṣis protected the amṛta, and with due permission of Śrī Brahmā, Pṛthvī Devī took the amṛta. She became the disciple of Śrī Brahmā. She left after taking the nectar."

Brahma Purāṇa:

In the one-hundred-sixth chapter of Brahma Purāṇa, we find the story of Samudra Manthana. This story has some unique elements, while its basic narrative is common. The story unfolds as follows:

"The devatās and asuras wanted to attain eternal life. So they concluded that they needed the nectar of life, Amṛta. They decided to churn the ocean to obtain the Amṛta. They made Mount Mandarāñchala the churning rod and Nāga Vāsuki the rope and started the process. After this, the Survallabha Amṛta came out. When they obtained the Amṛta, both parties decided to wait for a highly auspicious time to drink it.

When the asuras went away, the devatās thought it was not wise to share the nectar of life with their enemies. The devatās then asked their guru, Bṛhaspati, 'Where should we go to drink the nectar?' As they searched for a safe place, a cave of Mount Meru was chosen, and Hari was made the gatekeeper. Sūrya was the only one who truly understood the worth of the nectar. So, he informed Hari about whom to allow entry into the cave where the devatās were seated, drinking the Amṛta.

Rāhu knew this fact, so he went to the group of Maruts, where he successfully drank the Amṛta. Sūrya saw and recognised Rāhu, and informed Viṣṇu about it. Viṣṇu beheaded him with his chakra, but by then, he had already drunk the Amṛta, gaining immortality. Although his head was separated, he remained alive. His headless body fell on the southern bank of the Gautamī River.

At the request of the devatās, Śiva sent Caṇḍikā along with Mātṛkās to destroy the body of Rāhu. Īśvarī, a form of Śivaand Śakti, separated the nectar from Rāhu's body and destroyed it. As Rāhu had drunk the nectar, he was placed as a shadow planet in Jyotiṣa. The nectar separated from his body was stored in a Kumbha, from which a stream of Amṛta flowed, which came to be known as the River Pravara. Later, Ambikā also drank that nectar."

Viṣṇu Purāṇa:

Viṣṇu Purāṇa provides a backstory to why the devatās wanted to have the nectar, because of which they did such hard work. It says that once, Sage Durvāsā gave Devarāja a garland of flowers. He placed it around the neck of Airāvata, his royal elephant, who threw it again and crushed the garland underfoot. Sage Durvāsā, who saw it himself, became angry at the disrespect.

Sage Durvāsā, angrily, cursed Indra that all the wealth of his kingdom would be lost. When it happened, Indra went to Brahmā, who took him to Viṣṇu. Viṣṇu said to the devatās to take the asuras into their favour and perform Samudra Manthana in the Kṣīra Sāgara, which was his abode.

After making Mount Mandarāñchala a churner and Nāga Vāsuki as the rope, they churned the sea. The items they got here are different from what is mentioned in other Purāṇas:

Kāmadhenu, Kalpavṛkṣa, apsarās, candra, viṣa, and then Dhanvantari with the Amṛta Kalaśa at last. Viṣṇu gave the Kalaśa to the devatās.

Skand Purāṇa:

The Skanda Purana, the largest of all the Puranas, mentions the same story, albeit with a different version. It unfolds the narrative in the same way as in the prior section, but changes in the latter half. It says that.

"When Dhanvantari came out with the Kalaśa, Indra forcibly took the Kalaśa filled with nectar. Asuras took from Indra and went to the Pātāla-loka. At the request of Devatās, Viṣṇu went to Pātāla in his Mohinī form and took Amṛta from the Asuras. She gave it to the Devatās. Rāhu sat in the line of Devatās. Thus, he became immortal, but still, he was beheaded by Viṣṇu when informed by Sūrya."

Conclusion:

Purāṇa are the most sacred source of knowledge from ancient times. Written by Maharshi Veda Vyasa, also known as Krsna Dvaipayan, they stand at the centre of Indian mythology. In this chapter, we have glanced at one of the three foundational bases of the Kumbha celebration—the Paurāṇika stories. As mentioned earlier, these stories form the basis of the Kumbha celebration. However, one notable point is that the Purāṇas do not mention Kumbha being celebrated as a Melā in Haridvāra, Prayāga, Nāśika, or Ujjayinī at intervals of four years. Some folklore and additional narratives have been merged with the original Paurāṇika records, which are not found in the written texts.

In the case of Samudra Manthana, Kumbha is celebrated because, according to folklore, the Kumbha of Amṛta was carried by Jayanta, leading to a great struggle. During that struggle, drops of Amṛta fell at four locations, thus giving rise to the Kumbha celebration. As Jayanta, the son of Purandara Indra, held the Kumbha or Kalaśa in his hands and the Deva-Asura Saṅgrāma continued for twelve days of the Devatās—both on Earth and beyond—the Kumbha is celebrated at intervals of twelve years. This is because the complete solar revolution of Earth around the Sun is equivalent to one solar day of Svarga-loka.

In another narrative, the story of Kumbha-sthāpana by Garuḍa, folklore suggests an additional reason for the four Kumbha sat at four distinct locations. It is believed that while carrying the Amṛta from Svarga to his loka to free his mother from the slavery of Kadru, Garuḍa rested at four places. These locations later became the sites of the Kumbha celebrations.

Thus, we have now examined all versions of the stories from various Purāṇas and folklore. We shall now proceed to the next chapter, where the philosophical perspectives of these stories are discussed.

4. A Philosophical Insight

*The Sūrya, being a significator of Atman, is eternal,
while Candramā is the significator of the fickleness of
mind.
Bṛhaspati, being the Guru of the Devatas, represents
knowledge,
being the facilitator of Mokṣa or liberation.
Liberation for human beings is possible
when the mind aligns with the soul,
and the intellect becomes stable.
As Bṛhaspati is the giver of intellect,
he only bestows it in the best way
in his rāśīes— Vṛṣa, Singh and Kumbha, when the mind
and intellect, along with the atman,
the path of Mukti happens.*

This excerpt from Kumbha: Aitihāsika Vaṅgmaya by Heramb Chaturvedi, published in 2019 on the occasion of Prayāga Ardha-Kumbha, is a remarkable text that offers a philosophical perspective on Kumbha. Kumbha, in my view, is a congregation—the event on the planet —that delivers an unfathomable message about the path to liberation.

Millions of people spend their last penny just to be present during these special dates. This signifies their innate desire to be part of something larger—mokṣa (liberation). People seek something beyond their ordinary perception, something they cannot observe in normative conditions. The essence of the Purāṇas and other sacred texts is mokṣa. Thus, it is no exaggeration to say that the divine force attracting people to these holy lands is their inherent, conscious or unconscious, inclination towards liberation.

Liberation, in simple terms, is the attainment of the ultimate consciousness. It is believed that the Ātman is true consciousness. Moreover, Indian philosophical thought posits that matter is nothing but energy, energy is nothing but the jīva, and the jīva is the supreme source of energy. Thus, the yearning for freedom from pain, worry, fear of death, and the desire for an eternal life of bliss is the most fundamental aspiration of all beings. Though this requires persistent effort, the time of Kumbha makes the path significantly easier.

The Philosophy in the Kumbha:

There is a very popular verse in Sanskrit that talks about the spirituality of the Kumbha in great detail.

कलशस्य मुखे विष्णुः कंठे रुद्रः समाश्रितः।

मूले त्वाऽस्थितो ब्रह्मा मध्ये मातृगणाः स्मृताः॥

कुक्षौ तु सागराः सर्वे सप्तद्वीपा वसुधरा।

ऋग्वेदोऽथ यजुर्वेदः सामवेदो ह्यथर्वणः।

अंगैश्च सहिताः सर्वे कलशं तु समाश्रिताः।

अत्र गायत्री सावित्री शांतिः पुष्टिकरी तथा।

आयांतु देविपूजार्थ दुरितक्षयकारकाः॥

गंगे च यमुने चैव गोदावरि सरस्वती।

नर्मदे, सिंधु, कावेरि जलेऽस्मिन् सन्निधिं कुरु॥

श्रीवरुणाय नमः।

सर्वोपचारार्थे गंधाक्षतपुष्पाणि समर्पयामि॥

"In the mouth (opening) of the kalāśa (pot) is Lord Viṣṇu, in the throat is Lord Rudra (Śiva), at the base, is Lord Brahmā, and in the middle, the Mother Goddesses are invoked. In the stomach (or inside the pot), all the rivers, the seven continents, and the earth are present. The Ṛgveda, Yajurveda, Sāmaveda, and Atharvaveda are all present along with their respective limbs (branches). These Vedas sanctify the kalāśa. In this, the Gāyatrī mantra, Sāvitrī, Śānti (peace), and Puṣṭikārī (nourishment) are invoked. May they all come for the worship of the Goddess and the destruction of sins. May the divine rivers Gaṅgā, Yamunā, Godāvarī, Sarasvatī, Narmadā, Sindhu, and Kāverī be present in this holy water. O Lord Varuṇa, I bow to you. For all types of rituals, I offer sandalwood paste, rice, and flowers."

The Philosophy in the Story:

The Kumbha is closely related to the story of Samudra Manthana, in which the Adhidaiva forms play significant roles, such as Bṛhaspati, Sūrya,

Candramā, Rāhu, Ketu, and others. This concept was discussed in the previous chapter. Out of the three key aspects, the third point is elaborated in this chapter—how the Adhidaiva forms embody the characters in the narrative of Samudra Manthana.

The story of Samudra Manthana is not merely a historical event that occurred in the past and has lost its relevance in modern times. This is not the case with the Kumbha and the Purāṇika narratives associated with it. These stories will always hold significance for humanity, as they encapsulate profound interpretations of the human experience.

In a spiritual sense, the Kumbha is a revelation of a much larger concept that applies to our everyday lives. This concept unfolds through the understanding that the material body—known in Indian philosophy as the sūkṣma śarīra (subtle body)—is essentially an embodiment of the sūkṣma śarīra, the energy body in life. Within the sūkṣma śarīra, there exist seventy-two thousand nāḍīs, which are the pathways of energy flow. Among them, the Iḍā and Piṅgalā are the two most crucial nāḍīs. Additionally, there is a third and most significant nāḍī, known as Suṣumṇā.

In Yogic tradition, the ascension of energy from the Mūlādhāra Cakra to the Sahasrāra Cakra is regarded as the path to attaining ultimate consciousness. The relation of this process to the story of Samudra Manthana lies in the fact that the awakening of Suṣumṇā Nāḍī is akin to the churning of Mandarācala. Furthermore, the abode of Dhanvantari is within our hearts. Bṛhaspati, the guru of the devas, is the bestower of intellect. Sūrya represents the Ātman, while Candramā symbolises the Mana (mind).

In this context, Mohinī Viṣṇu represents Māyā—the distractions of the material world. Rāhu and Ketu correspond to the emotions of rāga (attachment) and dveṣa (aversion), and thus, they obscure Sūrya, the significator of Ātman, and Candramā, the symbol of Mana. Both good and bad exist in everyone's life; only the intensity varies. The struggle for dominance between these opposing forces continues throughout one's lifetime.

Now, analysing this story in the case of Prayāgarāj is a practical analysis of the above theory. In Prayāga, the Gaṅgā is the Iḍā; the Yamunā is the Piṅgalā, while the invisible Sarasvatī is the Suṣumnā Nāḍī. They all meet at the point of the Third Eye, which is the Triveṇī Saṅgama. Those who take a holy dip at this Triveṇī realise a deeper sense of truth.

इडा भगवती गङ्गा पिङ्गला यमुना नदी।

इडापिङ्गलयोर्मध्ये सुषुम्ना च सरस्वती॥

त्रिवेणी संगमो यत्र तीर्थराजः स उच्यते।

तत्र स्नानं प्रकर्त्तव्यं सर्वपापैः प्रमुच्यते॥

(Jñāna Saṅkālinī Tantra 11, 12)

These are said to be tīrthas. Tīrtha means "one who liberates." The path of liberation can be attained when one utilises the natural elements present around them appropriately. The human body, like all other bodies on Earth, is approximately 60% to 70% water. The other constituents include— 12% earth, 6% air, 4% fire, and 6% ākāśa. The dominance of jala(water) is evident in the human body. The same is true for pṛthvī (earth), which is 72% water. This reinforces the claim of Indian manīṣā—yathā piṇḍe tathā brahmāṇḍe— as absolute.

Thus, if we wish to maintain our body as a whole properly, we need to cleanse it in all available aspects. There are different types of tīrthas, but a common prerequisite for any place to be a tīrtha is the availability of water.

यथा शरीरस्योदेश्या: केचिन मेध्यात्मा: स्मृता: ।

यथा पृथिव्यामुद्देश्या: केचित् पुण्यतमा: स्मृता: ॥

प्रभावाद्द्धुताद् भूमे: सलिलस्य च तेजसा ।

परिग्रहान् मुनिनां च तीर्थानां पुण्यता स्मृता ॥

(Śabda-Kalpa-Druma Part 2)

One of the basic demands of any place to be a Tīrtha is that there must be the presence of a water body. This special importance given to Jala (water) is due to two fundamental reasons. Firstly, it is the very source of life. Not only does life originate from Jala, but it is also impossible to sustain without it.

In the Indian tradition, a Tīrtha can be associated with any of the five elements (Pañcamahābhūta)—earth (Bhū), water (Jala), fire (Agni), air (Vāyu), or space (Ākāśa). The ancient Indian belief that life emerged from water, or jala, has now been validated by modern science.

सोऽभिध्याय शरीरात्स्वात्सिसृक्षुर्विविधा: प्रजा: ।

अप एव ससर्जादौ तासु वीर्यमवासृजत् ॥

(Manusmriti 1.8)

"Desiring to create the several kinds of created things, he, in the beginning, by mere willing, produced, out of his own body, Water; and in that he threw the seed."

44

Scientific Significance of Kumbha

Kumbha, or the science of utilising the confluence of rivers at specific latitudes, is the result of keen observation of how fundamental forces constitute the basic elements of existence.

In the case of Prayāga, even the geographical situation is unique. During the month of Māgha, the Sūrya and the Earth come into closer proximity, as does the Candramā. As they draw nearer to the Earth, they exert significant influence on the water bodies, such as the Gaṅgā and the Yamunā. Since these three celestial bodies play a crucial role in the phenomenon of Kumbha, it is evident that the water bodies also undergo a substantial transformation during this sacred period. This transformation not only purifies the manah (mind) but also facilitates spiritual elevation.

It is a fact today that the planets have their electromagnetic fields. These fields have a significant effect on human life. A common example is the influence of the Candramā (Moon) on oceanic tides. On Pūrṇimā (Full Moon) and Amāvāsyā (New Moon), the sea experiences high tides, and this phenomenon is also observed in the human body. Most individuals who attained spiritual enlightenment did so on the day of Pūrṇimā. A prominent example is Gautama Buddha.

Regarding Gautama Buddha, Paṇḍita Jawāharlāl Nehrū wrote in The Discovery of India:

"It is stated in Buddhist literature that Buddha was born on this full moon day of Vaiśākha

(May–June); that he attained enlightenment and finally died also on the same day of the year."6

The menstrual cycle is also in synchronisation with the phases of the Candramā. This signifies that human beings exist in complete harmony with the external natural world. With future scientific discoveries, it will become evident that these ancient Indian beliefs are not merely traditional myths but rather a highly advanced, scientifically envisioned system.

The Yaugic Interpretation:

In the story of Samudra Manthan, Śiva drank the Kalkūt Viṣa. It was a deadly poison, but he drank it, and his neck turned blue; thus, one of his names is said to be Neelkanth.

One special interpretation is that he drank the poison and remained unaffected. In the Mahābhārata, it is said that he stopped the poison in his neck only. Had it entered the body of Śiva, it could have caused some harm, but it was stopped at the neck.

The story weaves a beautiful narrative, and the yogic culture explains it as the neck is the seat of the Vishuddhi Chakra. Vishuddhi is a chakra that means "one who purifies" in literal terms. This was the reason that, although he drank Viṣa, which is a cause of death, he spoke the Rāma Kathā Amṛta, by which Kak Bhūṣuṇḍī is still alive from the last 27 Kalpas.

---

6 *Footnote: Nehrū, Jawāharlāl. The Discovery of India. Oxford University Press, Delhi, 1946, p. 120.*

This story highlights that when the Vishuddhi Chakra is properly activated, it can help us detoxify from the toxic influences of the external world—whether it be harmful thoughts, emotions, or even physical substances. This purification process is vital for spiritual growth, and Śiva's ability to contain the poison within his throat can be seen as an embodiment of this purifying force.

The Message of Kumbha:

The message of Kumbha in the applied fields is surely the message that we humans are social animals. The concept of social collectivism, or saṅghau śakti kaliyuge, is brought to light by the people.

The idea is presented in the story that during the Samudra Manthan, both kinds of people came together—the devatās and the asuras—and they combined their efforts to obtain the nectar of life, which would make them eternal and bring them joy. We, humans, are also the people who need to come together and make the idea of the Vedas a living reality.

The Kumbha, in this sense, gives a resemblance to the fact that it is a festival that paves the path for one to come beyond this saṅkrānti or amalgamation of the nectar and viṣa, good and bad, win and defeat, gain and loss, and so on…

When one, with persistent effort, overcomes these torments of the mind, they attain the position of a sthiti-prajña, or one who remains unaffected by situations.

प्रजहाति यदा कामान्सर्वान्पार्थ मनोगतान्।
आत्मन्येवात्मना तुष्टः स्थितप्रज्ञस्तदोच्यते॥
(Bhagavad Gītā 2.55)

The Supreme Lord said: O Pārtha, when one discards all selfish desires and cravings of the senses that torment the mind, and becomes satisfied in the realisation of the self, such a person is said to be transcendentally situated.

Additionally, a festival that embodies a collective approach to various races, cultures, regions, traditions, sampradāyas, and more. In the view of samastī or aggregate, it envisions the idea of ekaḥ sute sakalam to the common people. This couplet of Goswāmī Tulasīdās from Rāmcaritmānas deeply resonated with this idea of Kumbha.

माघ मकरगत रबि जब होई। तीरथपतिहिं आव सब कोई॥
देव दनुज किन्नर नर श्रेणी। सादर मज्जहिं सकल त्रिवेणी॥
(Rāmcaritmānas 1.43.2)

He writes that not only humans but the devatās, kinnaras (a deva yonī which has a human torso with the horse body or horse torso with a human body), and all other species come to this land of Triveṇī Saṅgama. In traditional terms, everyone comes to the Kumbha—the devatās, the ṛṣis, munis, sādhus, bhūtas, prets, piśācas, Gandharvas, and all the species. This is what Goswāmī Tulasīdās said in the special reference to Triveṇī Kumbha.

Conclusion:

The Indian tradition of attaining knowledge of Brahman in its true sense has been revered since the Vedic ages. The Pūrṇa Kumbha symbolised knowledge in ancient Vaidik India. Thus, Kumbha is not merely a fair on the planet but also a profound revelation of truth.

An anecdote from Swami Ramakrishna Paramahamsa holds great significance in this context. He used to say:

"When a Kumbha is empty and submerged in water, it produces a sound. However, when it is filled to the brim, it remains silent. The same holds for humans. As long as we are not filled, we are full of doubts and questions. But once we are filled, there are no questions, no doubts. We become Pūrṇa Kumbha—whole and at peace."

5. An Analysis of Jyotiṣa

Many Indian newspapers have published an anecdote about the 1942 Prayāga Kumbha. When Lord Linlithgow (the then Viceroy of India) and Paṇḍit Madan Mohan Mālavīya saw the lakhs of people at the 1942 Melā, Linlithgow wondered how much money was spent on publicity to gather so many people. "Two paise," Paṇḍit Mālavīya replied. When a shocked Linlithgow asked Mālavīya how it was possible, Mālavīya took out a pañcāṅga and told him that it cost two paise to print a pañcāṅga, from which common Hindus would know when the Melā would be held, and nobody sent any invitations. I do not know if such a conversation took place between Linlithgow and Mālavīya, but the fact that no invitations are sent to the lakhs of sādhus, kalpavāsīs, and tīrthayātrīs attending the Melā is undeniable.

This excerpt from the chapter' Immortal Melā' from the book 'Kumbha' by Nityānanda Miśra mentions the relevance of Pañcāṅga in the context of Kumbha Melā and other special religious festivals of the Sanātana ethnicity.

The kāl or time, along with the deśa or land, are the two basic constructs in the Indian Jyotiṣa. The kāl is even one of the main seven pillars that provide the basis for the Pṛthavi.

धर्मः कामश्च कालश्च वासुर्वासुकिरेव च।
अनन्तः कपिलश्चैव सप्तैते धरणीधराः॥

(Mahābhārata
Anuśāsan Parv 150.41)

The Sanātana Vaidika tradition has four Vedas at its apex—Ṛk, Yajur, Sāma, and Atharva. Along with this, there are four Upavedas affiliated with each of them, namely Āyurveda, Dhanurveda, Gāndharva Veda, and Tantra or Sthāpatya Veda, respectively.

ऋग्यजुः साम चाथर्वा वेदा आयुर्धनुः क्रमात्।
गांधर्वश्चैव तन्त्राणि उपवेदाः प्रकीर्तिताः॥

(Śukra Nīti 4.3.27)

In the Yājñavalkya Smṛti, fourteen schools of knowledge are mentioned, including the four Vedas, the Vedāṅgas (the six limbs of the Vedas), the Purāṇa, Nyāya, Mīmāṁsā, and Dharmaśāstra.

पुराणन्यायमीमांसा धर्मशास्त्रांगमिश्रिताः।
वेदाः स्थानानि विद्यानां धर्मस्य च चतुर्दश॥

(Yājñavalkya Smṛti 1.3)

52

In the Ṣaḍaṅga, the six limbs are: Śikṣā, Vyākaraṇa, Kalpa, Nirukta, Jyotiṣa, and Chanda. This can be seen in the below śloka, which is as follows:

शिक्षा व्याकरणं कल्पो निरुक्तं ज्योतिषं तथा।
छंद: षडंगानीमानि वेदानां कीर्तितानि हि॥

(Śukra Nīti 4.3.28)

Jyotiṣa:

Jyotiṣa is the discipline of the Vedas that helps us determine the kāla suitable for performing Vaidika karma-kāṇḍa. From ancient times, Jyotiṣa has been the foundation of the Indian calendar, known as the Pañcāṅga, which remains accurate to the finest detail. This knowledge is made possible through Jyotiṣa, as formulated by great astronomers of ancient India, such as Āditya or Gargācārya.

This discipline, which enables us to understand tithi, nakṣatra, yoga, muhūrta, karaṇa, and the motion of grahas, is divided into three skandas (parts), namely—Saṁhitā, Horā, and Gaṇitā.

तिथिनक्षत्रयोगानां मुहूर्तकरणात्मकम्।
कालस्य वेदानार्थं तु ज्योतिर्ज्ञानं पुरानघ॥

(Mahābhārata 14.92 Dakṣiṇātya)

There is a story that highlights the benefits of carefully utilising kāla and deśa in one's actions. One who aligns their deeds with the appropriate time and place gains special advantages due to their conjunction.

परीक्ष्यकारी युक्तश्च स सम्यगुपपादयेत्।
देशकालावभिप्रेतौ तोभ्यां फलमवाप्नुयात्॥

(Mahābhārata 12.137.24)

In ancient times, Diti desired two mighty sons from her husband. Being a pativratā, she requested Ṛṣi Kaśyapa to bless her with children. However, he refused, as it was Sandhyā-kāla, during which such actions were prohibited. Ignoring his advice, she insisted and bore two sons—Hiraṇyakaśipu and Hiraṇyākṣa—who became the most formidable demons of their era. This story highlights the significance of kāla, as even a pativratā woman's disregard for proper timing resulted in severe consequences.

The timing of the celebration is also determined for Kumbha, as discussed in earlier chapters. In this chapter, we will explore the planetary aspects of Kumbha and its auspicious timings, referencing the Bṛhaspati, Sūrya, Candramā, and other important planetary motions and situations.

The Planetary Motions:

The Kumbha is celebrated every twelve years because it is always related to the cycle of the Bṛhaspati (Jupiter). For a better understanding, let us first understand the basics of Jyotiṣa to proceed to the further sections.

The Jyotiṣa divides the complete sky into twelve sections, each called a Rāśi, namely—Meṣa, Vṛṣabha, Mithuna, Karkaṭa, Simha, Kanyā, Tulā, Vṛścika, Dhanuṣ, Makara, Kumbha, and Mīna. There are nine planets, namely—Sūrya, Candra, Maṅgala, Budha, Bṛhaspati, Śukra, Śani, Rāhu,

KUMBHA

Ketu. Each planet has its own speed and position in the solar system. For example, the moon completes one revolution in 27.32 days, the sun completes one revolution in 365.2425 days, and Jupiter completes one revolution in 11.8618 years. Thus, this also means that one planet resides in one Rāśi for a short period and will return to the same Rāśi after a fixed time. Therefore, Kumbha is the eleventh Rāśi in the sky. When Bṛhaspati enters the Kumbha Rāśi, and special planetary conjunctures are there, it will surely cause the conditions necessary for the Kumbha.

As stated, the solar year comprises 365 days, 6 hours, 8 minutes, and 15 seconds, calculated based on the Sun's time to complete one full revolution across all the rāśis. In contrast, Bṛhaspati (Jupiter) takes 361 days, 1 hour, 20 minutes, and 34 seconds to traverse only one rāśi. This creates a difference of 4 days, 4 hours, 47 minutes, and 40 seconds between the solar year and the Bṛhaspati saṁvatsara. Over a cycle of twelve years, this difference accumulates to about 50 days, 8 hours, 43 minutes, and 47 seconds. As a result, after 86 years, Bṛhaspati will have advanced by one rāśi, reaching it about 16 days before the completion of the corresponding solar year. To put it simply, for the first seven consecutive 12-year cycles, Bṛhaspati will align with the rāśis in a way that matches the solar reckoning. But in the eighth cycle, the discrepancy becomes prominent: Bṛhaspati will arrive in its designated rāśi already in the 11th year, causing the Kumbha festival to be celebrated one year earlier.

This very discrepancy created considerable confusion in the celebration of the Kumbha festivals in recent history. The 1956 Siṁhastha Kumbha at

Ujjayinī and the 1953 Māghastha Kumbha at Prayāgraj witnessed disputes regarding the correct year of observance. A similar situation had also arisen earlier during the 1865 and 1866 Prayāgraj Kumbhas, where the difference between the solar reckoning and Bṛhaspati's movement led to the festival being celebrated in two consecutive years. To resolve this longstanding issue, Pūjya Svāmī Hariharānanda Sarasvatī (Svāmī Karpatrījī Mahābhāga) intervened. He convened a grand dharmasabha—a traditional assembly of scholars and saints to deliberate upon matters of Dharma. After a thorough discussion, the astronomical and scriptural facts outlined earlier were accepted as authoritative. The outcome was the compilation of a definitive treatise, Dharmakṛtyopayogī Tithyādinirṇayaḥ Kumbhaparvanirṇayaśca, a text that has since served as the standard reference for resolving any date-related disputes concerning the Kumbha festival.

There are some important days in the festival of Kumbha, known as Śahi Snān, when the Akhāḍās gather to bathe and celebrate it collectively. Some of them are like Makar Sankranti, Mauni Amavasya, and Vasant Panchami.

Kumbha in Haridwār:

The sacred Haridwar, also known as Gaṅgādwār, is a town situated on the banks of the Gaṅgā, and we have discussed the city in detail in the previous chapter.

The Kumbha in Haridwār is celebrated on the banks of Har ki Paurī, also known as Shiva's feet. This is the deśa of the place in Jyotiṣa, one of the two aspects, the other being kāl. Let us now explore the

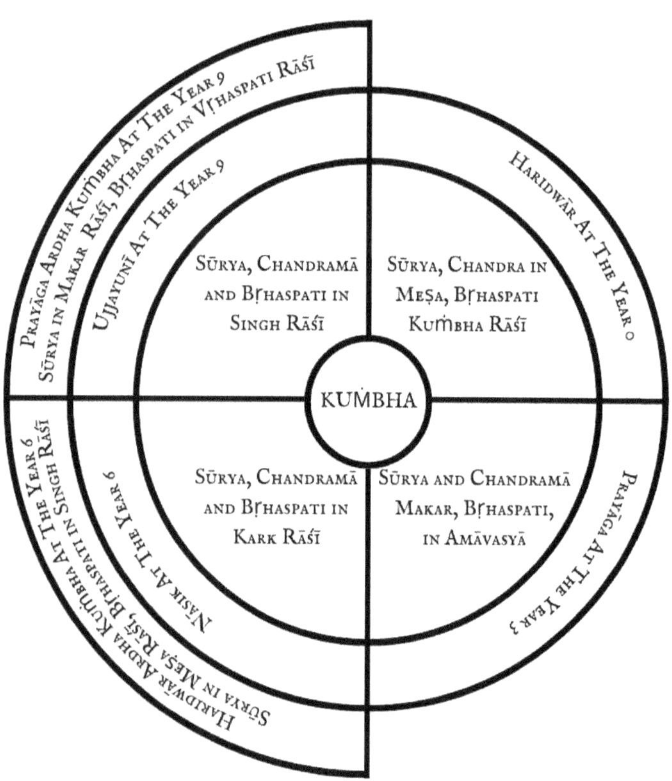

Table 1: A cyclic order Kumbha, along with Ardha Kumbha.

kāl in the context of Kumbha.

The Kumbha Melā is held in Haridwār when Bṛhaspati (Jupiter) is in Kumbha Rāśi (Aquarius) and the Sūrya (Sun) is in Meṣa (Aries).

पद्मिनी नायके मेषे कुम्भ राशिगते गुरुः ।

गंगा द्वारे भवेयोगः कुम्भ नामा तदोत्तमाः ॥

कुम्भ राशि गते जीवे यद्दिने मेषगोरविः ।

हरिद्वारे कृतं स्नानं पुनरावृत्ति वर्जनम् ॥

(Skand Purāṇa)

The Sūrya usually enters Meṣa in Phālguna, but the Haridwār Kumbha of 2010 and the Ardha Kumbha of 2016 are both instances of this, and this is the kāl of the Haridwār Kumbha. Now, we know both aspects, being kāl and the deśa.

The special śahi snān days of the Haridwār Kumbha are:

- **Mahā Śivaratri**: Mahā Śivaratri is celebrated on the 14th night of the kṛṣṇa pakṣa in the month of Phālguna (usually in February or March).

- **Chaitra Amāvāsya**: Chaitra Amāvāsya is observed on Amāvāsya (new full moon day) in the month of Caitra according to the Hindu lunar calendar. This day usually falls in March or April.

- **Meṣa Saṅkrāntī**: It is also known as the Baishākhī Saṅkrāntī, the name of the month. Mesha Sankrānti marks the entry of the Sūrya into the zodiac sign of Meṣa (Aries) and is considered the start of the Hindū solar new year. This festival is celebrated on April 14th or 15th every year, depending on the exact timing of the Sūrya's entry into Meṣa.

Every sixth year, the Ardha Kumbha is celebrated in Haridwār and also in Prayāga.

Kumbha in Prayāga:

The sacred Prayāga, also known as Prayāgarāja, is a town situated on the confluence of the Gaṅgā, Yamunā, and Sarasvatī rivers. We have discussed the city in detail in the previous chapter.

The Kumbha in Prayāga is celebrated at the Triveni Saṅgam, the confluence of the three rivers: the Gaṅgā, the Yamunā, and the Sarasvatī, which is often considered a hidden River. This represents the deśa aspect in Jyotiṣa. The other crucial aspect is kāla. Let us now explain the kāla aspect of the Kumbha.

The Kumbha Melā is held at Prayāga when Bṛhaspati (Jupiter) is in Vṛṣa (Taurus) and Sūrya (Sun) is in Makara(Capricorn).

मेष राशिगते जीवे मकरे चन्द्र भास्करौ।

अमावस्यां तदा योग कुम्भाख्य तीर्थनायके॥

मकरे च दिवानाथे हय्जगे च बृहस्पतौ।

कुम्भ योगो भवेत्तत्र प्रयागे ह्याती दुर्लभ: ॥

(Skand Purāṇa)

The Prayāga Kumbha is celebrated for two months, beginning from Makara Saṅkrānti and culminating on Mahā Śivarātri.

In the case of Kumbha, the three most auspicious days for śāhi snān are:

• **Makara Saṅkrānti:** When Sūrya enters Makara (usually on the 13th or 14th of January).

- **Maunī Amāvāsya:** The Amāvāsya of the Māghā month, which falls in late January or February.

- **Vasanta Pañcamī:** The Pañcamī, the fifth day of the śukla pakṣa of the Māghā month.

Additionally, the Māgha Melā is celebrated annually during the month of Māgha, coinciding with the Kumbha and Ardha Kumbha, which occur every **twelve years** and **six years**, respectively.

Kumbha in Nāsik-Trayambakeśwar:

The Kumbha on the banks of Godāvarī is celebrated at two specific sites: Nāsik and Trayambakeśvara. The former is primarily for Vaiṣṇavas, while the latter is dedicated to Śaivas. Despite this distinction in worship traditions, both sites share the same kāla for the Kumbha Melā.

Thus, Rāma Kuṇḍa in Nāsik, situated on the banks of the Godāvarī, represents the deśa aspect of Kumbha in Jyotiṣa. Now, let us delve further into the kāla aspect.

The Kumbha Melā is held on the banks of the Godāvarī when both Sūrya (Sun) and Bṛhaspati (Jupiter) are in Siṃha(Leo). This is why the Nāsik Kumbha is also known as the Siṃhāstha Kumbha.

सिंहराशि गते सूर्ये सिंहराशौ बृहस्पतौ।
गोदावर्य्या भवेत्कुम्भः पुनरावृत्तिवर्जनम्॥

(Skand Purāṇa)

When Sūrya and Bṛhaspati are both in Siṃha Rāśi, the Kumbha Melā is celebrated on the banks of the Godāvarī River.

The Nāsik-Trayambakeśvara Kumbha is observed for approximately two months, typically from July to September.

The three most auspicious days for the śāhi snāna at Kumbha Nāsik are:

- **Śrāvaṇa Pūrṇimā:** The Pūrṇimā of the Śrāvaṇa month, which is celebrated as Rakṣābandhana (usually in August).

- **Bhādrapada Amāvasyā:** The Amāvasyā of the Bhādrapada month.

- **Ṛṣi Pañcamī:** The Pañcamī, or the fifth day of the bright half (śukla pakṣa) of the Bhādrapada month.

A significant site in Nāsik is Rāma Kuṇḍa, where the Gaṅgā-Godāvarī Mandir opens only during the Kumbha Melā. The temple was last open from July 14, 2015, to August 12, 2016, and will reopen again in 2027.

Kumbha in Ujjayunī:

The sacred Ujjayinī is a town located on the banks of the Shipra, and we have discussed the city in detail in the previous chapter.

The Kumbha Melā is held in Ujjayunī on the banks of the Śiprā when Sūrya (Sun) is in Meṣa (Aries) and Bṛhaspati(Jupiter) is in Siṁha (Leo). This is the deśa aspect of Jyotiṣa. The other aspect is known as kāla. Let us now explain the kāla aspect of the Kumbha.

When any planet is in Siṁha Rāśi, it is said to be siṁhāstha. Since Bṛhaspati is Siṁhastha when the Ujjayunī Kumbha is held, it is also known as Siṁhastha Kumbha.

मेषराशिगते सूर्य सिंहराशौ बृहस्पतौ।
उज्जयिन्यां भवेत्कुम्भ: सर्वसौख्य विवर्धन: ॥
मेषराशिगते सूर्ये सिंहराशौ बृहस्पतौ।
कुम्भयोग स विज्ञेय: भुक्ति-मुक्ति प्रदायक: ॥

Meaning: "When the Sūrya enters Meṣa and Bṛhaspati is in Siṁha, the Kumbha occurs in Ujjayunī. It is always the bestower of liberation."

The Ujjayunī Kumbha is the shortest among all four Kumbha Melās, lasting only one month. It is held during April and May, two of the hottest months in Ujjayunī and India.

At Ujjayunī Kumbha, the three most auspicious days for the śāhi snāna are:

• **Chaitra Pūrṇimā:** The Purṇimā of the Chaitra month and the first day of the Melā.

• **Akṣaya Tṛtīyā:** The third day of śukla pakṣa of the Vaiśākha month.

• **Vaiśākha Pūrṇimā**: The Purṇimā of the Vaiśākha month and the last day of the Melā.

Conclusion:

The Kumbha has been celebrated with great enthusiasm every year for thousands of years. The people come to the specific deśa and kāl without any prior invitation. However, we observe some differences in the dates of the Kumbha, such as the Prayāga Kumbha of 1965 and 1966. Furthermore, the subtle variations in the cycles of time and planetary alignments create a unique spiritual experience each time the Melā is held. This interplay between cosmic rhythms and earthly rituals is what gives the Kumbha its timeless significance. Each celebration, whether at Prayāga, Haridwar, Nashik, or Ujjainī, carries its own set of divine energies, inviting devotees to embark on a sacred journey of purification and renewal. Though the outer manifestations may differ, the essence remains constant—a collective pilgrimage of devotion, reflection, and transcendence. The Kumbha, therefore, is not merely a festival but a profound spiritual occurrence that transcends time and space, connecting the past, present, and future in a sacred embrace.

6. Historical Perspective

Ādi Śaṅkarāchārya travelled to Prayāga to engage in a śāstrārtha (philosophical debate) with Kumārila Bhaṭṭa, a renowned karmakāṇḍī-mīmāṁsaka and a conqueror of Buddhist scholars. Upon arriving, Śaṅkara found that Kumārila had set himself on self-immolation at Triveni Saṅgama to atone for betraying his teacher. Kumārila had once been a Buddhist disciple, learned both Vaidik and Buddhist texts, and defeated the Buddhists; however, he felt guilty for his betrayal. Śaṅkara urged him to come out of the fire to converse, but Kumārila humbly declined, as his lower body was already burned. He then directed Śaṅkara to Maṇḍana Miśra, who would later become his disciple, Sureśwarāchārya.

This excerpt from the Śaṅkara Digvijaya by Vidyāraṇya highlights the significance of Prayāga, a Kumbha site, even during Śaṅkarāchārya's time. While the historicity of Triveṇī is well-established by evidence and historians, it does not directly confirm the history of the Kumbha Melā. Although Triveṇī and the Akṣaya Vat are notable features of the region, there is no clear historical reference to the Kumbha Melā being held at Prayāga, Haridwar, Nāṣik, Ujjain, or on the banks of the Gaṅgā, Śiprā, or Godāvarī.

The written records about very ancient events are not available to us. As India is a continuous civilisation, many aspects of that time may have been lost or destroyed throughout history. In 2008, Kama Maclean published her work, Pilgrimage and Power: The Kumbha Melā in Prayāgaraj, 1954-1965, through Oxford University Press. Her primary focus was the sociological aspects of the Kumbha. She claimed that the Kumbha as a Melā originated after British rule in India. Although there appears to be a lack of concrete evidence supporting the existence of the Kumbha Melā in ancient records, substantial evidence suggests that such gatherings were indeed evident in the Indian subcontinent. Maclean's assumption could stem from conflating the Kumbha Melā with the Magh Melā held annually in Prayāgaraj during the Indian month of Magh (usually from January to February). This annual gathering aligns with the timing of the Kumbha Melā, which occurs once every twelve years. However, in the other three locations—Haridwar, Ujjain, and Nashik—the Magh Melā or the provision of Kalpavāsa is not observed. Thus, in her work, she rejected the vast ancient records that indicated the existence of the Kumbha Melā through the lens of history.

KUMBHA

The records of the conflicts between Haridwār Kumbha in the eighteenth century and the shifting of the Kumbha site for Vaiṣṇavas to Rāma Kuṇḍa, due to the interference of the Pēṣwā, are two common historical figures that refute the basic assumption of Kama as a false basis. Was this a result of neo-colonial historiography, or was she biased by her cultural lens?

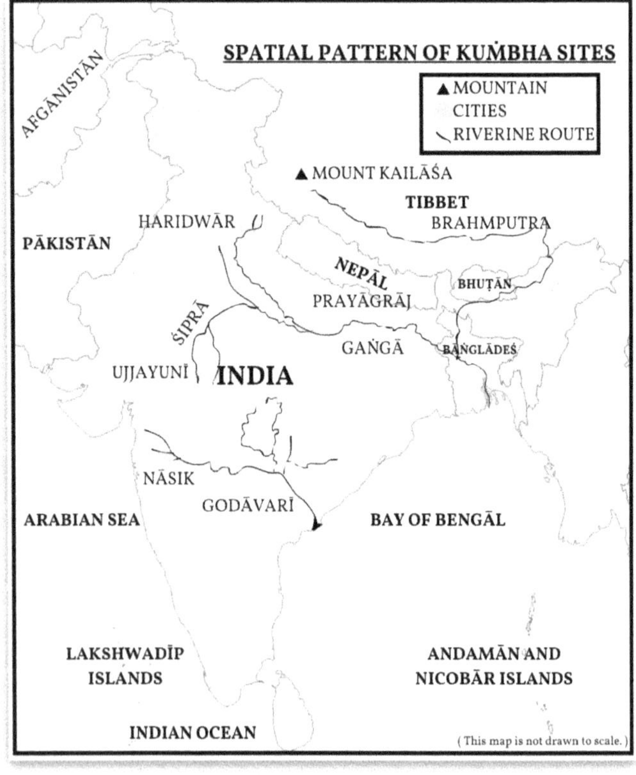

Map 1: The sites of Kumbha in India

The ancient records of Kumbha were either lost or destroyed. A significant portion of this loss can be attributed to foreign invasions and the consistent attempts to undermine Indian historiography. What was left from all the calamities was taken to England by the British as an artefact for their museum!

The Greek traveller Megasthenes was sent as an ambassador to India by Seleucus Nicator to the court of Cāndragupta Maurya. On his way to Magadha, he stayed for 75 days in Prayāga, vividly narrating the city and its glory in Indica.

Fa-Hien, a Chinese scholar who visited India from 399 to 411 CE, wrote extensively about the Buddhist sites at Vārāṇasī and Kaushāmbī, but did not mention the city of Prayāga. This omission can be attributed to two possible reasons: First, it could be assumed that Prayāga was not settled during that time, though this is not true, as the city and the Trivenī Saṅgama are mentioned in Buddhist texts. The second and more likely reason is that Fa-Hien was primarily interested in Buddhist sites, which led him to focus on places like Kaushāmbī, a flourishing capital at the time, while bypassing other regions.

It is not until the later Gupta period that we encounter mention of Prayāga in the writings of Xuanzang, who visited India from 629 to 645 CE. In his book, Buddhist Records of the Western World, he records:

> "Once in five years, he held the great assembly called mokṣa. He emptied his treasuries to give all away in charity."

This statement strongly indicates that the ArdhaKuṁbha was being celebrated at that time. When the ArdhaKuṁbha is observed, it implies the existence of the full Kuṁbha Melā as well. Xuánzàng even mentions that Buddhist scholars participated in the gathering alongside brāhmaṇas, highlighting the inclusive and diverse nature of the congregation.

The great Hindu philosopher and saint, Ādi Śaṅkarācārya of the 6th century BC[7], is traditionally credited with formalising the Kuṁbha Melā. He intended to establish major gatherings for śāstrārtha (philosophical discourse) and debates among the Hindu monastic community. These congregations aimed to consolidate and strengthen the intellectual foundations of Sanātana Dharma, fostering a sense of unity and shared purpose among its practitioners. He used the age-old Kuṁbha festival as a social gathering to revitalise Vaidik traditions, organise monastic orders, and play a crucial role in preserving and propagating Advaita Vedānta. But in the śāstras, it is mentioned that the tradition of Kuṁbha was older than Ādi Śaṅkarācārya himself. By the time the Akhāḍās came into existence, they had acquired this tradition on a greater scale. Over a significant period, they evolved into great institutions, serving as guiding forces at the Kuṁbha Melā.

---

[7] *While mainstream historians have long placed Ādi Śaṅkarācārya Mahābhāga in the 8th century CE, this dating does not align with the latest research by several Indian chronologists—such as Vedaveer Ārya—who argue for a significantly earlier period, a view also supported by scholars adhering to traditional historical accounts..*

In the thirteenth-century India, Jadunāth Sarkār, in his book The History of Daśnāmī Nāgā Sanyāsīs, mentions a turning point in the history of Kumbha when, in Haridwār, the Sanyāsīs achieved victory over the bairāgīs in the thirteenth century CE.

Neville, in his District Gazetteer Of The United Provinces of Āgrā and Oudh, published in 1909, mentions that in the year 1398 CE, Tīmūr had massacred a large number of Hindu devotees in Hardwār. In the same century, historical records document a significant description of the melā or fair at the confluence of the Gaṅgā, Yamunā, and Sarasvatī rivers in Prayāga.

In the medieval period, a grand festival at Prayāga is mentioned in the Ain-i-Akbarī. Abū'l-Fazl writes in his book on page 158:

"Illahabād, anciently called Prayāg, was distinguished by His Imperial Majesty by the former name. A stone fort was completed, and many handsome edifices were erected. The Hindus regard it as the King of Shrines. Near it, the Gaṅgā, the Yamunā, and the Sarasvatī meet, though the latter is not visible. Near the village of Kantal, considerable captures of elephants are made. What is most strange is that when Jupiter enters the constellation Leo, a small hill appears from the Gaṅgā and remains there during the space of one month, in which the people offer divine worship."

As with other notable sources, even Abū'l-Fazl is reluctant to use the name of the congregation. Another book, Tabaqat-i-Akbari, authored by Nizamuddīn Ahmad, mentions a great fair organised in Prayāga during the month of Māgha. While these sources did not use the term Kumbha, the first instance of Kumbha with the name Kumbha in official records is found in two sixteenth-century books: Khulāsatu-T-Tārīkh by Sujan Rai Bhandārī and Chahār Gulśan written by Rāi Caṭar Man

Kayāth. Both of these books belong to the reign of Auraṅgzeb in seventeenth-century Mughal India.

In the Khulāsatu-T-Tārīkh, the author mentions the Kuṁbha at Haridwār:

"In short, this river, having come out of the hill of Badri, reaches the foot of the city of Śrīṅgar, the residence of the king of that country. From there, it passes by Hariśikheśa and issues from the hill at Hardwar. Should be worshipped from its origin to its end, yet Hardwar is described as the greatest of all holy places on its banks. Every year, on the day when the sun enters the sign of Aries, which is called Baisākhī, people from every side assemble here; especially in the year when Jupiter enters the sign of Aquarius (otherwise named Kuṁbha), which happens once every 12 years, vast numbers of people assemble here from remote distances."

Another book mentions, Chahār Gulśan, about the Haridwār Kuṁbha as:

"Melā at Hardwar in Baisākha: the largest gathering takes place in the year in which Jupiter enters the sign of Aquarius, and is called the Kuṁbha melā. Lacs of laymen, Faqīrs, and Sanyāsīs assemble here. If any Faqīrs of Prag [or Bairāgī?] come here, they are attacked by the Sanyāsīs."

The Vaishnavite Bhakti Literature provides evidence that Caitanya Mahāprabhu visited Prayāga in 1514, during the Magha Melā. According to the literary evidence, he met his two brothers on this occasion, and they became disciples of Caitanya Mahāprabhu.

māgha-māsa lāgila, ebe yadi yāiye
makare prayāga-snāna kata dina pāiye[8]

---

[8] *The Bengali text from Caitanya Caritāmṛta, 18.145:*
মাঘ-মাস লাগিল, এবে যদি যাইয়ে।
মকরে প্রয়াগ-স্নান কত দিন পাইয়ে॥

It is also worth stating that Vallabhācārya met Caitanya Mahāprabhu in a boat on the river Yamunā, and had been with him in his āśrama at Arail, Prayāga.

G. S. Ghurye, in his book Indian Sādhus, mentions two books of different periods, both of which state that the Kumbha takes place at two sites. The first book, authored by Gangādhara Sarasvatī in the fifteenth century, is named Gurucaritra and mentions the celebration of the Simhastha Kumbha Melā at Nāsik. The other was a Pārsī text, Dabistān-i-Mazāhib, which contained records of the Kumbha Melā of seventeenth-century Haridwar.

Mahant Rādhāmohan Dāsa Jī of Nāsik possessed a copperplate inscription, as mentioned by Subhas Rāi in his book Kumbha Melā: History & Religion, Astronomy, Cosmo-Biology, that mentions a great massacre of Bairāgīs that took place in 1690 CE at Nāsik.

According to the Jhānsi Gazetteer, in 1751, Ahmad Khān Bangās, after defeating the Nawab of Awadh, Sūbdarjān, attempted to capture the fort of Prayāga. But at that time, the Kumbha at Prayāga happened, and a group of Nāga ascetics came to Prayāga under the leadership of Śrī Rajendra Gīrī. Firstly, they performed their rituals and then fought from February till April, eventually defeating the forces of Ahmad Khān Bangās.

In 1938, the British government passed the United Province Melās Act, which gave the Magha Melā equal importance to that of the city administration.

Conclusion:

The history of the Kumbha Melā is a fascinating tale of religious unity, cultural continuity, and historical transformation. From its ancient origins, with early mentions by foreign travellers like Megasthanes and Xuánzàng, to the detailed accounts provided by scholars and chroniclers like Abū'l-Fazl and Sujan Rai Bhandari, the Kumbha stands as a testament to the resilience and vibrancy of Indian spiritual and social traditions. It reflects the evolution of Hinduism from a largely localised practice to a pan-Indian and even global phenomenon, drawing millions of devotees from all walks of life to witness the grandeur of the event.

The Kumbha Melā, with its association to sacred geography—Prayāga, Haridwār, Nāṣik, and Ujjain—has symbolised not just the convergence of rivers but the confluence of time, space, and spirituality. From the role of Ādi Śaṅkarācārya in institutionalising the Kumbha through monastic orders and the rise of Akhāḍās, to the struggles for supremacy between different sects and the conflicts witnessed in the Melā, this chapter has illustrated the multiple layers of history embedded in the celebrations.

The Kumbha Melā has continuously adapted to the socio-political context of its times. From invasions to colonial rule, the festival and its associated traditions endured. The disruption of the festival's practices during foreign invasions and the shifting of sites, such as the change in the site at Ram Kund in the 18th century, speaks to the dynamic nature of the Kumbha, even as it preserved its sacred essence. The fact that the Kumbha continues to thrive today, as a symbol of communal harmony and devotion, despite the passage of centuries, speaks volumes about the vitality of Indian traditions.

Ultimately, the Kumbha Melā is much more than just a religious event; it is a cultural phenomenon, a historical marker, and a living tradition that continues to shape the spiritual and social landscape of India. As the Kumbha unfolds every twelve years, it serves as a poignant reminder of the enduring power of faith and the ability of ancient traditions to evolve and endure through time.

7. The Akhāḍās

*Most of the Nāgas belong to the Daśnāmi Sampradāya,
organised by Śaṅkarācārya, the oldest, largest, and most
effective of our monastic Orders.
On initiation, the Daśnāmi, as the very name indicates,
is given a name combined with one of the ten words:
Giri, Puri, Bhāratī, Van, Araṇya, Parvat, Sāgar, Tīrtha,
Āśrama or Sarasvatī. The initiate has to make strict
vows not to indulge in more than one meal a day; not to
beg for food from more than seven houses; not to sleep
anywhere but upon the ground; not to salute, not to
praise, nor speak ill of anyone; not to bow to anyone but
a sannyāsī of a higher order; not to cover himself with a
cloth, unless it were a bhagwā brownish-red color.*

This excerpt from The History of Dashnami Naga Sanyasis, authored by Jadunāth Sarkār with a preface by Kanhaiyā Lāl Munśī, makes a profound mention of Nāgā Sanyāsī. Let us now delve deep into the Akhāḍās and see their role and involvement in the Kumbha. No work about the Kumbha can be completed without the mention of the Akhāḍās and their importance in this congregation. In this chapter, let's delve into the Akhāḍās, their introduction, historicity, classifications, and participation in Kumbha, particularly in the context of the modern era.

Introduction to Akhāḍas:

The term Akhāḍa translates to "arena", symbolising a place for rigorous training and preparation for ascetics. This training traditionally encompasses Śāstra Vidyā (knowledge of weapons) and Śāstra Vidyā (knowledge of spiritual and religious texts). Within Akhāḍās, ascetics strive for proficiency in both, with Śāstra Vidyā—spiritual wisdom and religious knowledge—forming the essence of their practice.

Akhāḍās serve as vital institutions for nurturing and sustaining Hindu Dharma. They are centres of Ādhyātmik Jñāna (spiritual knowledge), guiding seekers on their path to enlightenment. Beyond spiritual education, Akhāḍās support society in upholding Dharma through rites and ceremonies such as births, sacred thread initiations, and marriages. They also organise Bhaṇḍāras (mass feeding events), fostering community welfare.

By preserving age-old traditions and practices, Akhāḍās act as custodians of India's spiritual and cultural legacy, ensuring festivals like Kumbha remain vibrant and deeply rooted in their original ethos.

The practices within an Akhāḍa emphasise sādhana (spiritual disciplines) such as intense meditation, scriptural study, chanting, and rituals aimed at self-realisation and spiritual wisdom. These practices foster discipline, selflessness, and devotion. Members also undergo rigorous training to attain mastery in spiritual knowledge while cultivating detachment and humility.

Akhāḍās embody a harmonious balance between spiritual pursuit and societal responsibility. Renouncing worldly life and possessions, their members actively contribute to preserving and enriching Indian traditions. Their sādhana elevates their spiritual growth while inspiring others to walk the path of Dharma, making Akhāḍās pillars of India's timeless spiritual heritage.

Historical Background

The system of Akhāḍās in India is ancient, with a long-standing tradition of wrestlers who were once patronised by royalty. During the time of King Kaṁsa, wrestlers like Cāṇūra and Muṣṭika, who enjoyed royal favour, fought in the Akhāḍās. Their famous encounter with Kṛṣṇa in the wrestling arena, where they were defeated, culminated in the death of Kaṁsa by Kṛṣṇa himself. This incident signifies that Akhāḍās, as wrestling arenas, have existed in India for centuries, long before they became spiritually associated with ascetic traditions.

The concept of Akhāḍās as spiritual centres only emerged when the Indian subcontinent began to face external threats, particularly from the western borders. In response to these growing challenges, the Śaṅkarācārya of the four Pīṭhasrecognized the need for a spiritual force to protect India's culture and traditions. Thus, they initiated the formation of Daśnāmi Akhāḍās, groups of ascetics with one of ten distinctive names that marked their affiliation to this order. These names are: Giri (mountain), Puri (city), Bharati (Bharat), Tīrtha (pilgrimage), Van (forest), Araṇya (wilderness), Parvat(mountain), Āśrama (sacred space), Sāgara (ocean), and Sarasvatī (goddess of knowledge).

Each of these names represented a specific domain of protection. For instance, Giri protected hills, Purī safeguarded urban centres, Bhāratī upheld the without bondage, Tīrtha protected sacred sites, Van ensured the preservation of forests, Araṇya looked after deep forests, Parvat took care of mountain ranges, Āśrama protected sacred spaces, Sāgara safeguarded water bodies, and Sarasvatī preserved knowledge and learning.

Primarily, these Akhāḍās consisted of ascetics associated with the Śaṅkara sect, dedicated to preserving India's cultural and spiritual heritage. Over time, they became instrumental in defending not just the physical aspects of India's culture but also its soul and traditions.

Akhāḍās have played a pivotal role in the four Kuṁbha Melās, ensuring their vibrancy and continuity. They also fought to protect India's temples, cultural institutions, and traditions, often challenging Islamic and British dominance during critical historical periods. Their involvement in the Kuṁbha festivals and their role as protectors of India's rich heritage make them indispensable pillars of the nation's spiritual foundation.

Classification of Akhāḍas

The akhāḍas were not built overnight. Their step-by-step approach paved the way for the creation of such a great institution. The Śankarācārya akhāḍas were among the first to be established and are thus the most ancient akhāḍas of all time, still guiding the religion.

There are three types of akhāḍas, traditionally prevalent among the Śankara sect:

1.   **The Śaiva or Daśanāmī akhāḍā**

2.   **The Vaiṣṇava akhāḍā**

3.   **The Udāsīn akhāḍā**

The Śaiva or Daśanāmī akhāḍas are the akhāḍas of sannyāsīs, including Mahā-nirvāṇī, Aṭal, Nirāñjanī, Ānand, Jūnā (Bhairava), Avāhan, and Agni. The Vaiṣṇava akhāḍas comprise three sub-sects: the Digambara, Nirmohī, and Nirvāṇī akhāḍas. The Udāsīn akhāḍas include Udāsīn Pañcāyatī Baḍā akhāḍā and Udāsīn Pañcāyatī Nāyā akhāḍā.

1.   **Avāhan Akhāḍā:**
     The akhāḍā is said to be the oldest akhāḍā, dated to Vikram Saṁvat 603, which corresponds to 547 CE. Eminent Jadunāth Sarkār of the twentieth century writes in his book The History of Daśnāmī Nāgā Sanyāsīs that—
     "Hira Bhāratī, Siddha Gudarbal Bhāratī planted the banner, Ganpat Bhāratī blew the trumpet. Hardwar Bhāratī built the akhāṛā. Vikram Samvat 603, Jyeṣṭha Kṛṣṇa Pakṣa 9th, Friday (If the figure for one thousand has been

omitted before the year, as used to be done in old writings, such as Portuguese official records, then the year would be 1603 V.S.—1547 CE.)"

Thus, there is a possibility of both interpretations, i.e., this could be in the year 547 CE or 1547 CE[9]. The iṣṭa of this akhāḍā is Gajānana and Dattātreya, while it is affiliated with the Jūnā Akhāḍā. While its headquarters is in Kāśī, the other centres are in Prayāga and Haridwār.

2. **Aṭal Akhāḍā:**
This akhāḍā, formed by the combined efforts of fifteen sādhus, was established on the land of Gondvāna. It was founded on the Caturthī of Śukla Pakṣa in the Mārgaśīrṣa month of the Indian calendar, which corresponds to 1647 CE in the official government records.

In a historical context, this akhāḍā is known for having defeated the army of Bundelā warriors. Their iṣṭa is Gaṇeśa, while its

---

[9] *Jadunāth Sarkār set a precedent by recording that the years of initiation of the akhāḍās were counted only after the dating of Ādi Śaṅkarācārya was fixed in the 7th century CE. Consequently, all akhāḍās whose origins predated the 7th century CE were said to be a millennium ahead in his book The History of the Daśnāmi Nāgā Sannyāsīs. However, in many cases, akhāḍās formed in more recent times did not omit the millennium in their dates, which indicates that Sarkār's system is not universally applicable. Moreover, it is implausible that these akhāḍās were influenced by Portuguese calendrical conventions at the time. Now, with the conclusion that Ādi Śaṅkarācārya lived in the 6th century BCE, it is reasonable to argue that the akhāḍās in his authentic line were indeed ancient, corresponding to years such as 603 V.S. (547 CE).*

headquarters are in Kāśī, though it was earlier located in Jodhpur. It is affiliated with the Mahānirvāṇī Akhāḍā. Their main weapon is the spear, known as Sūryaprakāśa or Candraprakāśa.

3. **Nirvāṇī Akhāḍā:**
Established by Śrī Śivakaraṇa in Vikram Saṁvat 805, corresponding to 748 CE, its main deity (iṣṭa devatā) is Kapila. The prominent siddha nāgās, such as Rūpa Giri Siddha, Uttama Giri Siddha, Rāmasvarūpa Giri Siddha, Śaṅkara Puri, and Pūrṇānanda Bhāratī Agnihotrī, among many others, were skilled in both śastra vidyā (knowledge of weapons) and śāstra vidyā (spiritual and scriptural knowledge).
They even fought and proved their skills in the Gaḍhkuṇḍā of Jharkhaṇḍa. It is even said that they fought against Aurangzeb's army in 1664 on behalf of Kāśī Jñānavāpī and successfully defeated his forces.

4. **Ānanda Akhāḍā:**
With the support of the Barār regions, it was founded in the year Vikram Saṁvat 912, which corresponds to 856 CE. However, if the logic of Jadunāth Sarkār is applied here as well, the year would be 1912 Vikram Saṁvat or 1856 CE. The exact tithi corresponds to the Pañcamī of Śukla Pakṣa of the Jyeṣṭha month, which fell on a Sunday.
It was established in the Vidarbha Kṣetra of Mahārāṣṭra. Like the prior two akhāḍās, this one is affiliated with the Nirañjanī Akhāḍā. Their iṣṭa devatā is Sūrya. Their headquarters are in Haridwar, while other important centres include Kashi, Nashik, Prayag, and Ujjaini.

5. **Niranjanī Akhāḍā:**
Many sannyāsīs gathered in the Maṇḍavī of Kaṭcha. This Akhāḍā was established in the year 1960 Vikram Saṁvat on the Ṣaṣṭhī of Kṛṣṇa Pakṣa, which fell on a Monday. This translates to 1904 CE. The iṣṭa devatā of this Akhāḍā is Kārtikeya. Currently, its headquarters are in Prayāgrāj, while its other centres are in Kāśī, Haridwār, Oṁkāreśvara, Ujjayinī, Tryambakeśvara (near Nāśika), and Udayapura.

6. **Jūnā Akhāḍā:**
It was established in Karṇaprayāga, Uttarakhaṇḍa, in the year 1202 Vikram Saṁvat, which corresponds to 1146 CE. Among the founders were Bhokhama Giri, Sundara Giri, Maunī, Digambara, Dalpata Giri Nāga, Nīlakaṇṭha Bhāratī, Śaṅkara Purī, and Benipurī Avadhūta. The main deity (iṣṭa devatā) of this Akhāḍā is Dattātreya, and its headquarters are located at Hanumān Ghāṭa, Kāśī.

7. **Agni Akhāḍā:**
Among the Akhāḍās of the Śaṅkara Daśanāmī Paramparā, Agni Akhāḍā is the last. Established in the year 1112 Vikram Saṁvat on Āṣāḍha Ekādaśī, it primarily affiliates brahmacārīs of the Daśnāmī Akhāḍā Paramparā.

Now, let us have a look at the Vaiṣṇava Paramparā:

1. **Nirmohi Anī:**
This Akhāḍā has eight sub-sects within itself, namely—Rāmānandī Nirmohi, Rāmānandī Mahānirvāṇī, Rāmānandī Santosī, Harivyāsī

Mahānirvāṇī, Harivyāsī Santosī, Viṣṇu Svāmī Nirmohi, Māḷādhārī Nirmohi, Rādhāvallabhyā Nirmohi and Jhaḍīyā Nirmohi

2. **Digambara Anī:**
It consists of only two sub-sects: Rāmjī Digambara and Śyāṃjī Digambara

3. **Nirvāṇī Anī:**
It has seven sub-sects under it. They are: Rāmānandī Nirvāṇī, Niralambī, Rāmānandī Khākī, Harivyāsī Khākī, Harivyāsī Nirvāṇī, Bālabhadrī and Tātāmbārī

Out of the total eleven Akhāḍās, seven Akhāḍās are devoted to Śrī Rāma, and the remaining five are dedicated to Śrī Kṛṣṇa.

The Udāsīn Akhāḍas are indeed rooted in the Sikh tradition, closely aligned with the teachings of Guru Nānak Dev and emphasising spiritual disciplines like renunciation, meditation, and devotion. These Akhāḍas are part of the broader tradition of Udāsīnī, which rose around the 15th century to address the growing spiritual and social needs of the time.

Here's a closer look at both sects within the Udāsīn Akhāḍa:

1. **Udāsīn Pañcāyatī Baḍā Akhāḍā**
. This is one of the more prominent branches of the Udāsīnī tradition. Known for its deep spiritual practices, it stresses detachment and renunciation. It is dedicated to the worship of Śrī Rāma and holds a significant place in the Vaiṣṇava paramparā, contributing to the continuity of ascetic practices and spiritual learning. The Baḍā Akhāḍā focuses on

maintaining the purity of its practices while promoting community welfare and upholding the ideals of simplicity and spiritual awakening.

2. **Udāsīn Pañcāyatī Nāyā Akhāḍā**
. This branch represents a newer evolution within the Udāsīnī sect. While sharing similar core values, it leans towards a more localised and practical approach to ascetic life. It specifically emphasises the worship of Lord Kṛṣṇa as a central figure in its devotional practices. The Nāyā Akhāḍā is recognised for its dynamic, grassroots spiritual outreach and its commitment to fostering a deeper connection with local communities through meditation, social service, and spiritual teachings.

Both Akhāḍas reflect the flexible nature of the Udāsīnī tradition and its capacity to adapt to different regions and practices while remaining faithful to the core principles of Sikh spirituality, which include devotion to God, service to humanity, and the pursuit of spiritual knowledge.

Participation in the Kumbha Melā

The Kumbha Melā is a centuries-old spiritual gathering that represents one of the largest and most significant cultural events in the world. Among the diverse participants, the Akhādas play a pivotal role in organising, guiding, and ensuring the spiritual sanctity of the Melā. Their active participation in the Kumbha Melā is a testimony to their historical importance in preserving the essence of Hindu Dharma.

At the heart of the Kumbha Melā, the Akhādas, with their centuries-old tradition of ascetic discipline and spiritual practice, serve as the backbone of this vast and complex religious event. They are the institutions that organise the major rituals, lead processions, maintain spiritual discipline, and contribute to the social and religious vibrancy of the Melā. They also serve as custodians of the ancient practices that have evolved over thousands of years. To fully understand the role of the Akhādas in the Kumbha Melā, one must look into their origins, functions, classifications, and involvement in this grand spiritual celebration.

The Kumbha Melā is not only a religious gathering but also a socio-cultural event that draws together a vast diversity of people, from ascetics to common folk. The Akhādas play a central role in ensuring that the Kumbha Melā remains a spiritually uplifting experience for all participants. They offer spiritual guidance, lead rituals, and create an environment that fosters reflection, devotion, and learning.

One of the most important roles of the Akhādas during the Kumbha Melā is the Shāhī Snān or royal bath. This ritual marks the most significant moment of the Melā, with thousands of sādhus from various Akhādas taking the ceremonial plunge into the holy river. The Akhādas participate by leading these baths in an orderly manner, with special privileges afforded to certain Akhādas based on their historical status and prominence.

The monastic akhāra and their Śrī Pañcha of various sects meet during the Kumbha Melā. The Nāga sādhus and various akhāras traditionally lead and initiate the bathing rituals, which are then followed by the general population.

The order of procession is as follows:

- **Mahānirvāṇī akhāra with Atal akhāra,**

- **Niranjanī akhāra with Ānand akhāra,**

- **Jūnā akhāra with Ahvāhan and Agni akhāra,**

- **Nirvāṇī akhāra,**

- **Digambar akhāra,**

- **Nirmohi akhāra,**

- **Nāyā Udasīn akhāra,**

- **Baḍā Udasīn akhāra, and**

- **Nirmal akhāra.**

Another important social role of the Akhādas is their involvement in community welfare activities. They organise mass bhandāras (free meals) for pilgrims, ensuring that no devotee goes hungry during the Melā. These efforts are not just acts of charity but embody the spirit of renunciation, humility, and service—key tenets of the ascetic lifestyle followed by Akhādas. The Akhādas also manage camps that provide accommodation, medical assistance, and spiritual guidance to the millions of pilgrims attending the Melā.

While the Akhādas have maintained their traditional roles in the Kuṁbha Melā, their participation has evolved. In the modern era, the Kuṁbha Melā has experienced exponential growth, attracting millions of devotees from around the world. This dramatic increase in the number of participants has compelled the Akhādas to adapt and innovate, striking a balance between tradition and modernity.

Technological advancements have played a significant role in the way Akhādas organise their activities at the Melā. The introduction of electronic platforms for communication, the use of digital technology for managing camps, and the facilitation of online donations are some of the modern advancements that have been incorporated to streamline operations and enhance the experience for both pilgrims and organisers.

Innovations brought in by the Akhādas have been pivotal in adapting to the demands of a rapidly evolving world. These developments have allowed the Akhādas to extend their influence beyond the Melā itself, ensuring that their teachings and practices reach a global audience.

With the rise of social media platforms, many Akhādas have embraced the power of the internet to share their spiritual messages, rituals, and discourses. Online lectures, live-streamed rituals, and virtual participation in bhandāras have enabled followers from all parts of the world to experience the sacredness of the Kumbha Melā, even if they are unable to attend in person.

Furthermore, the Akhādas have also incorporated technology into their traditional camps, utilising modern amenities to ensure better accommodation, cleanliness, and safety for the pilgrims. Electronic tracking systems for managing the vast crowds, along with improved medical facilities, have enhanced the overall experience of the Melā participants.

At the same time, the core values of the Akhādas—renunciation, devotion, discipline, and community service—remain unchanged. These eternal principles continue to guide the spiritual practices and interactions of the Akhādas, ensuring that, despite the technological advancements, the Melā remains grounded in its traditional ethos. The Kumbha Melā continues to be a deeply spiritual and communal experience, and the Akhādas remain its guiding force, ensuring that the Melā retains its sanctity and spiritual significance for generations to come.

Conclusion:

The Kumbha Melā is a celebration of India's spiritual heritage, and the Akhādās play a central role in this grand event. Their participation in the Melā is not merely ceremonial but is woven into the very fabric of the Melā's existence. From their historical significance as centres of spiritual practice to their modern role as leaders in community welfare, the Akhādas remain integral to the success and sanctity of the Kumbha Melā. The event, which draws millions of pilgrims, would not be the same without the Akhādas guiding the way through their rituals, teachings, and selfless service.

Through their unwavering commitment to Hindu Dharma and their adaptability in the face of changing times, the Akhadas continue to play a pivotal role in India's spiritual life, ensuring that the Kumbh Mela remains a timeless symbol of devotion, unity, and the eternal quest for spiritual enlightenment. Their participation in the Melā serves as a poignant reminder of the enduring power of faith, tradition, and community in shaping the nation's spiritual identity.

8. Conclusion

An analysis of the genesis, symbols and merits of the Kumbha indicates that the legendary Parva (Amrit Kumbha) and the Mela named after it presents inseparably two different aspects of Indian life. The attributes of the former refer to philosophical Kumbha that could only provide the spiritual benefits. The merits of the latter, on the other hand, are related to spatio-temporal bioeffects of the planetary radiations, particularly of sunspots, lunar phases and other cosmic bodies in conjunction with the bath benefits from the concerned rivers. To provide greater antiquity and validity to the latter, the mythological symbolisms of the former were attached with it, however, in course of time. In the confounded origin of the Kumbha, thus the elements of macrocosm, such as, planets, gods, demons, milk ocean, Kumbha sites, etc., represent their counterparts i.e. plexus and system in the microcosm (body) i.e. that involve in arousal of the serpentine power. Thus the legendary origin of the Amrit Kumbha refers to the arousal of serpentine power by celebrating the Kumbha Parva of the microcosm with the help of various elements. The Mela of the macrocosm, on the other hand, represents the scientific religion of Hindus.

This excerpt from Rai, Subhas. Kumbha Mela: History & Religion; Astronomy & Cosmobiology. Ganga Kaveri Publishing House, 1993, presents the Kumbha festival as a unique convergence of spiritual, cultural, and cosmic principles. The Kumbha Melā stands as a testament to the continuity of Indian civilisation, embodying an intricate synthesis of spirituality, tradition, history, and cultural evolution. This work traces its origins, significance, and evolution over time: what began as a sacred gathering for philosophical discourse and ritual purification has grown into the world's largest religious congregation, attracting millions of pilgrims from across the globe, while preserving the ancient symbolisms that link the macrocosm to the microcosm.

The study of Kumbha through a historical lens allows us to move beyond its mythological associations and perceive it as a dynamic tradition that has continuously adapted to socio-political changes. The journey from the Vaidik and Purāṇika references to the formalisation of the Melā under Ādi Śaṅkarācārya, the patronage of ruling dynasties, and its encounters with colonial forces reveals a layered history that cannot be reduced to a singular narrative. The Kumbha Melā has survived centuries of political turmoil, invasions, colonial disruptions, and even contemporary challenges, yet it remains an unshaken pillar of India's cultural and spiritual identity.

A Tradition Rooted in Antiquity

The origins of the Kumbha Melā are deeply intertwined with the ancient Indian worldview, in which time was perceived as cyclical rather than linear. The association of Kumbha with celestial alignments underscores the belief that human actions are deeply connected with cosmic rhythms. While mythological narratives such as Samudra Manthana provide a symbolic framework for its origins, historical inquiries lead us to another reality —that periodic religious congregations have been a hallmark of Indian civilisation for millennia.

Ancient Indian texts, including the Mahābhārata, Purāṇas, and accounts by foreign travellers, indicate that large-scale gatherings for religious and philosophical discourses were a common occurrence. The presence of Yajñas, mass pilgrimages, and ritual baths at sacred rivers suggests that the Kumbha Melā was not a sudden invention but rather a natural extension of long-standing traditions. These early references, however, do not explicitly mention the Kumbha Melā as we know it today, reinforcing the need to differentiate between the broader phenomenon of religious gatherings and the institutionalised Kumbha Melā.

The Role of Ādi Śaṅkarācārya and the Evolution of Akhāḍās

One of the most transformative moments in the history of Kumbha Melā was the contribution of Ādi Śaṅkarācārya in the 8th century CE. As a philosopher, reformer, and spiritual unifier, he sought to restore the declining influence of Sanātana Dharma by revitalising its monastic traditions. The establishment of four Maṭhas (monastic centres) in different corners of India aimed at reinforcing the spiritual and philosophical unity of Hinduism.

The Akhāḍās, which played a central role in shaping the Kuṁbha Melā, emerged as strongholds of monastic and martial discipline. Originally intended to safeguard dharma, these institutions became an integral part of the Melā, taking charge of rituals, processions, and maintaining order and discipline within the community. Their role expanded significantly during medieval times, particularly in response to external threats and invasions. This period marked the militarisation of Sādhus, as the Nāgā Sannyāsīs and other sects began taking up arms to defend sacred spaces.

The evolution of Akhāḍās from spiritual communities to organised institutions with distinct hierarchies and traditions underscores the adaptability of Kuṁbha Melā. What was once a purely spiritual gathering gradually took on a socio-political dimension, with different sects asserting their influence over ritual practices and territories within the Melā.

Colonial Interference and Modern Challenges

The arrival of colonial powers, particularly the British, marked a significant shift in the administration and perception of Kuṁbha Melā. The colonial rulers viewed such large gatherings as both an opportunity for revenue collection and a potential threat due to their sheer scale. While British officials documented the Melā extensively, their accounts were often coloured by a Eurocentric perspective that overlooked its deeper spiritual and historical significance.

Scholars like Kama Maclean, in her work Pilgrimage and Power: The Kumbh Melā in Allahabad, 1765-1954, suggest that the institutionalisation of Kumbha Melā as a Melā itself gained prominence only during colonial rule. However, this assumption overlooks the vast historical records and the deep-rooted presence of religious congregations in Indian tradition. The British may have attempted to regulate and categorise the Melā, but they did not create it. Their interference led to changes in its organisation, such as administrative structuring and the imposition of taxation on pilgrims, yet the spiritual essence of the Kumbha remained intact.

Even in post-colonial India, the Kumbha Melā continues to evolve, responding to modern technological advancements and infrastructure developments. Today, digital platforms facilitate pilgrimage planning, sanitation systems have improved drastically, and governance models have adapted to accommodate the growing influx of devotees. Yet, the essence of Kumbha—its spiritual vibrancy and collective faith—remains unaltered.

Symbolism and the Future of Kumbha Melā

The Kumbha Melā is more than just a gathering—it is a living tradition that embodies the principles of renunciation, devotion, purification, and unity. It serves as a reminder of India's ancient wisdom, where the material and the spiritual are harmoniously integrated. The ritual bath (Snāna), philosophical debates, ascetic practices, and communal living all represent different facets of an ideal society envisioned in Hindu philosophy.

In a rapidly modernising world, the relevance of Kumbha Melā extends beyond religious boundaries. It stands as a model for mass human congregation, offering insights into large-scale event management, environmental sustainability, and cultural diplomacy. The sheer organisational complexity of the Melā, which successfully accommodates millions within a limited timeframe, has been studied by scholars worldwide.

However, the Kumbha Melā also faces challenges. The increasing commercialisation of religious tourism, environmental concerns stemming from pollution in sacred rivers, and political influences shaping its narrative all pose questions about its future authenticity. While modernisation is inevitable, it is essential to ensure that the core spiritual values of the Melā are not diluted in the process.

Final Reflections

Reflecting upon the historical journey of Kumbha, we find that it is neither a rigid event nor a recent invention. It is an evolving phenomenon that has absorbed various cultural, political, and spiritual influences while maintaining its foundational essence. From the time of the Ṛṣis who gathered at sacred rivers for discourse, to the structured monastic assemblies of Ādi Śaṅkarācārya, to the resilience of Akhāḍās through medieval and colonial times, the Kumbha Melā has remained an unbroken link to India's spiritual consciousness.

The endurance of the Kumbha Melā over centuries signifies the resilience of Indian traditions in the face of adversity. It reaffirms that spirituality, when deeply embedded in culture, can endure over time and withstand transformation.

As we conclude this exploration, one thing remains certain—the Kumbha Melā is not merely an event; it is an experience, a legacy, and a testament to the undying spirit of faith. Whether viewed through historical, mythological, sociological, or philosophical lenses, the Kumbha Melā continues to inspire, unite, and purify those who partake in its sacred journey. And as long as rivers flow and seekers gather, the Kumbha Melā will continue to be a timeless symbol of India's spiritual heritage.

98

Glossary

1 *Ahaṅkāra* Ego or the sense of 'I' and 'mine,' a concept in Indian philosophy that ties an individual to material existence and prevents self-realization.

2 *Ākāśa* Ether or space, considered the first and most subtle element in the universe. It is one of the five elements (pañcabhūta), along with earth, water, fire, and air.

3 *Ānanda* Bliss or supreme happiness, often used to describe the ultimate state of joy that comes with self-realization or union with Brahman.

4 *Ānanda-maya-kośa* The sheath or layer of bliss, one of the five koshas (sheaths) in Vedantic philosophy that surrounds the soul, signifying the experience of pure joy and transcendence.

5 *Aśrama* A stage of life or place of retreat for spiritual practice. There are four aśramas in life: Brahmacarya (student), Gṛhastha (householder), Vānaprastha (retirement), and Sannyāsa (renunciation).

6 *Āśrama* A stage or a phase in life, such as Brahmacarya (student life), Gṛhastha (householder), Vānaprastha (retirement), and Sannyāsa (renunciation).

7	*Ātman*	The soul or self, representing the essence of an individual, which is eternal and transcends physical existence.
8	*Avidyā*	Ignorance or the lack of true knowledge, which is considered the root cause of suffering and the cycle of birth and rebirth in Hindu philosophy.
9	*Āyurveda*	The traditional system of medicine from India that focuses on balance in the body, mind, and spirit. It is based on the understanding of the three doshas: Vāta, Pitta, and Kapha.
10	*Bhakti*	Devotion or love for God, often practiced through prayers, rituals, and acts of service. It is one of the paths to spiritual liberation.
11	*Brahmā*	The creator god in Hinduism, who is responsible for the creation of the universe and all beings.
12	*Brahman*	The ultimate reality or cosmic spirit, formless, infinite, and eternal, which is the source of all creation and consciousness in Hinduism.
13	*Dharma*	The moral law and duty, which governs individual conduct, social responsibilities, and spiritual progress.
14	*Dhyāna*	Meditation or focused contemplation, often practiced to quiet the mind and connect with the divine or higher consciousness.

15 *Jñāna* Knowledge or wisdom, particularly spiritual knowledge that leads to the realization of the self and ultimate truth.

16 *Jyotiṣa* Vaidik astrology, which studies the influence of celestial bodies on human affairs and natural events. It is often used to explain the relationship between the cosmos and individual destinies.

17 *Kāla* Time, often personified as a deity in Hindu cosmology. Kāla represents both the cyclical nature of time and the destruction it brings.

18 *Karma* The law of cause and effect, where every action has consequences that affect an individual's future.

19 *Kṣetra* Field or sacred space, often used to describe a location or area that is imbued with spiritual significance, such as a pilgrimage site.

20 *Kumbha* Refers to a vessel or pot, often symbolising the container of cosmic knowledge, the self, or the universe in Vaidik and Paurāṇika contexts. The term also relates to astrological aspects and sacred rituals, particularly the Kumbh Melā.

21 *Līlā* Divine play or the concept of the universe being a manifestation of God's playful and spontaneous creation, often used in reference to the actions of deities like Krishna and Śiva.

22 *Mantra* — A sacred utterance or chant, often in Sanskrit, that holds spiritual power and is used in meditation, prayer, and rituals to invoke divine forces.

23 *Māyā* — The illusion or appearance of the material world, which obscures the true nature of reality and is tied to the concept of duality.

24 *Mokṣa* — Liberation from the cycle of birth, death, and rebirth (saṁsāra), attained through spiritual realization and union with Brahman.

25 *Paramātman* — The supreme soul or divine consciousness, often equated with God or the universal spirit in Hindu philosophy.

26 *Paurāṇika* — Refers to the Purāṇas, a genre of ancient texts that narrate the history of the universe, gods, and legends. These texts are considered as secondary scriptures, elaborating on the teachings of the Vedas.

27 *Prakāśa* — Light, often used metaphorically to signify knowledge, wisdom, or the presence of the divine.

28 *Prakṛti* — Nature or the material world, the feminine counterpart to Puruṣa, which is the source of all physical forms and manifestations.

29	*Prāṇa*	Life force or vital energy that permeates the body and the universe. In yoga and spiritual practices, controlling and directing prāṇa is key to attaining higher states of consciousness.
30	*Pūjā*	A ritualistic worship or offering to deities, which may include prayers, hymns, incense, and food offerings.
31	*Puruṣa*	The cosmic being or universal spirit, often represented as the primordial man, from whom the universe is created.
32	*Puruṣārtha*	The four aims or goals of human life: Dharma (righteousness), Artha (prosperity), Kāma (pleasures), and Mokṣa (liberation).
33	*Rāga*	Attachment or desire, often referring to emotional bonds and passions that bind an individual to material existence.
34	*Rajas*	One of the three gunas, associated with activity, passion, and desire. It is the force that propels action and change.
35	*Ṛṣi*	A sage or seer, typically a highly enlightened being who has attained spiritual insight and often composed hymns or mantras.
36	*Sādhanā*	Spiritual practice or discipline undertaken to achieve self-realization or attain spiritual goals.

37	*Śakti*	The divine feminine energy, considered to be the dynamic force behind creation, preservation, and destruction in the cosmos.
38	*Saṁsāra*	The continuous cycle of birth, death, and rebirth, driven by karma and ignorance (avidyā).
39	*Samskāra*	Rituals or rites of passage that purify the individual and prepare them for spiritual growth. It can also refer to mental impressions or conditioning accumulated from past actions.
40	*Samudra Manthana*	The churning of the ocean, a well-known Paurāṇika story in which the gods and demons churn the ocean to obtain the nectar of immortality, symbolising the eternal struggle between good and evil.
41	*Sattva*	One of the three gunas (qualities or attributes) in Hindu philosophy, associated with purity, goodness, harmony, and balance.
42	*Siddhi*	Spiritual powers or abilities that are acquired through intense meditation, self-discipline, or divine grace. They represent the attainment of higher knowledge and supernatural capabilities.
43	*Śiva-Śakti*	Refers to the divine pairing of Lord Śiva (the masculine, transcendental principle) and Goddess Śakti (the feminine, creative energy), often seen as complementary forces in Hinduism.

44	*Sṛṣṭi*	Creation or the process of manifestation of the universe. In your context, it refers to the creation of literary or metaphysical works that reflect cosmic principles.
45	*Sūtra*	A concise, aphoristic text or scripture that encapsulates profound spiritual teachings or concepts. The Yoga-sūtras of Patanjali is one example.
46	*Tamas*	One of the three gunas, associated with darkness, ignorance, inertia, and confusion. It is the quality that obstructs clarity and spiritual progress.
47	*Tantra*	Esoteric spiritual texts and practices that emphasize the worship of deities through ritual, meditation, and mantra chanting to achieve liberation.
48	*Upaniṣad*	A collection of ancient philosophical texts that explore the nature of reality, the self (ātman), and the ultimate reality (Brahman).
49	*Vaidik*	Pertains to the Vedas, the ancient sacred scriptures of Hinduism, which include hymns, rituals, and philosophical discourses.
50	*Vairāgya*	Renunciation or dispassion, especially with regard to material desires. It is a key quality for spiritual progress in many Indian philosophical traditions.

51	*Veda*	The sacred texts of Hinduism, consisting of the Ṛigveda, Yajurveda, Sāmaveda, and Atharvaveda, which contain hymns, mantras, and rituals.
52	*Vidyā*	Knowledge or learning, especially in a spiritual or philosophical context. It is often used to refer to sacred or higher knowledge.
53	*Viṣṇu*	One of the principal deities in Hinduism, known as the protector and preserver of the universe.
54	*Yajña*	A Vaidik ritual of offerings accompanied by chanting, performed to invoke blessings from gods and deities.
55	*Yuga*	An age or epoch in Hindu cosmology, representing a cycle of time. There are four main yugas: Satya Yuga, Treta Yuga, Dvapara Yuga, and Kali Yuga.

Bibliography

1. Chaturvedi, Heramb. Kumbh : Aitihasik Vangmaya. Vani Prakashan, 2019.

2. Maclean, Kama. Pilgrimage and Power: The Kumbh Mela in Allahabad, 1765-1954. Oxford UP, USA, 2008.

3. Megasthenes. Megasthenes' Indica: A New Translation of the Fragments with Commentary. Routledge, 2021.

4. Bharthrihari. Vakyapadiya. Chaukambha Sanskrit Series Office. 1961.

5. Nischalananda, Swami. Sahitya Darshan. Swasti Prakashan Sansthan. 2019.

6. Nischalananda, Swami. Jyotish Darshan. Swasti Prakashan Sansthan. 2019.

7. Shastri, Keshava Lal V. Upanishads in Three Volumes. Chaukhamba Sanskrit Pratishthan. 2021

8. Shastri, Bhimsen. Laghu Siddhanta Kaumudi - Bhaimi Vyakhya Part 1. Bhaimi Prakashan. 2013-2017.

9. Atri, Neeraj, and Munieshwar A. Saagar. Brainwashed Republic: India's Controlled Systemic Deracination. Abhishek Publications, 2017.

10.The Journal of the Royal Asiatic Society of Great Britain and Ireland, vol. 1895, no. 4. Cambridge University Press. 1895.

11.Tulasidas, Goswami. Shri Ram Charit Manas. Gita Gorakhpur. 2014.

12.Gandhi, M. K. The Story of My Experiments With Truth. Fingerprint! Publishing, 2020.

13.Sarkar, Jadunath. A History of the Dasnami Naga Sannyasis. 2018.

14.Ghurye, Govind Sadashiv. Indian Sadhus. South Asia Books. 1964.

15.Rai, Subhas. Kumbha Mela: History & Religion; Astronomy & Cosmobiology. Ganga Kaveri Publishing House. 1993.

16.Mishra, Nityananda. Kumbha: The Traditionally Modern Mela. Bloomsbury India. 2019.

17.Samuel Beal. Si-Yu-Ki: Buddhist Records of the Western World. Books for All. 2008.

18.Vidyaranya, Madhav. Shankar Digvijaya. 2013.

19.Shankaracharya, Adi. Discipline of Mathas in the Lineage of Shankaracharya. Swasti Prakashan Sansthan. 2012.

20.Trivedi, Ram Govind. Rigveda Samhita with Padapatha and Sayanabhasya (Set of 9 Volumes). Chaukhambha Vidya Bhawan. 2016.

21.Gaud, Pt. Ramswaroop Sharma. Atharva-Veda-Samhita Along with Sayana Bhasya (In Eight Volumes). Chaukhambha Vidya Bhawan. 2021.

22. Yajur-Veda-Samhita, Along with Sayana Bhasya (In Eight Volumes). Chaukhambha Vidya Bhawan. 2021.

23. Sam-Veda-Samhita, Along with Sayana Bhasya (In Eight Volumes). Chaukhambha Vidya Bhawan. 2021.

24. Prajnananan, Paramhamsa. Jnana Sankalini Tantra. Prajna Publication. 2004.

25. Hariharananda Saraswati, Swami. Marxvad Aur Ramrajya. Gita Press Gorakhpur. 2019.

26. Mishra, Jagdish Chandra. Shukra Niti. Vaidik Pustakalaya. 2022.

27. Hemchandra, Acharya. Anekarth Sangrah. Vidya Press. 2024.

28. Saraswati, Gangadhar. Shri Gurucharit. CreateSpace Independent Publication. 2018.

29. Nehru, Jawaharlal. The Discovery of India. Oxford University Press, Delhi. 1946.

30. Deva, Raja Radha Kanta. Shabdkalpdrumah. Chaukhamba Sanskriti Series Office, Varanasi. 1967.

31. Fazl, Abu'l. Ain-E-Akbari. Baptist Mission Press. 1878.

32. Ahmad, Khwajah Nizamuddin. Tabaqat-I-Akbari. The Asiatic Society. 2015.

33. Bhandari, Sujan Rai. Khulasatu-T-Tawarikh. J & Sons Press. 1918.

34. Kayath, Rai Chatar Man. Chahar Gulshan. 2007.

35. Manu, Maharshi. Manusmriti: DharmaShastra. Prabhat Prakashan. 2020.

36. Vyasa. Mahabharata. Gita Press Gorakhpur. 2017.

37. Vyasa. Mahabharata (Set of 9 Volumes). Chaukhamba Surbharati Prakashan, 2008.

38. Vyasa. Bhagavad Gita. Gita Press Gorakhpur.

39. Vyasa. Harivamsha Purana. Gita Press Gorakhpur.

40. Vyasa. Shri Bhagavata Purana. Gita Press Gorakhpur.

41. Vyasa. BrihanNaradiya Purana, Part 2. Chaukhamba Surbharati Prakashan.

42. Vyasa. Agni Purana. Chaukhambha Surbharati Prakashan.

43. Vyasa. Shiva Maha Purana. Gita Press Gorakhpur.

44. Vyasa. Devi Bhagavata Purana. Gita Press Gorakhpur.

45. Vyasa. Vishnu Purana. Gita Press Gorakhpur.

46. Vyasa. Varaha Purana. Gita Press Gorakhpur.

47. Vyasa. Garuda Purana. Chaukhamabha Surbharati Prakashan.

About the Author

Mayur Pandey, an author of Indian origin, has demonstrated his debut literary skills across various fields of literature in both Hindi and English. Currently pursuing his B.A. With a Saṁskrit Honours degree from Banaras Hindu University, he has showcased his talent through two published works, Prabhāt and Nav Ālok. These compilations of Hindi poetry encompass a diverse range of themes, including culture, nature, the Guru, poverty, marriage, and the pursuit of spiritual unity.

In this book, the author embarks on a quest to uncover a holistic understanding of the cultural ethos intricately woven into the fabric of Indian heritage. At the heart of this exploration lies Kuṁbha, the grandest festival, revered as a spiritual and cultural beacon of the timeless Sāraswat civilisation.

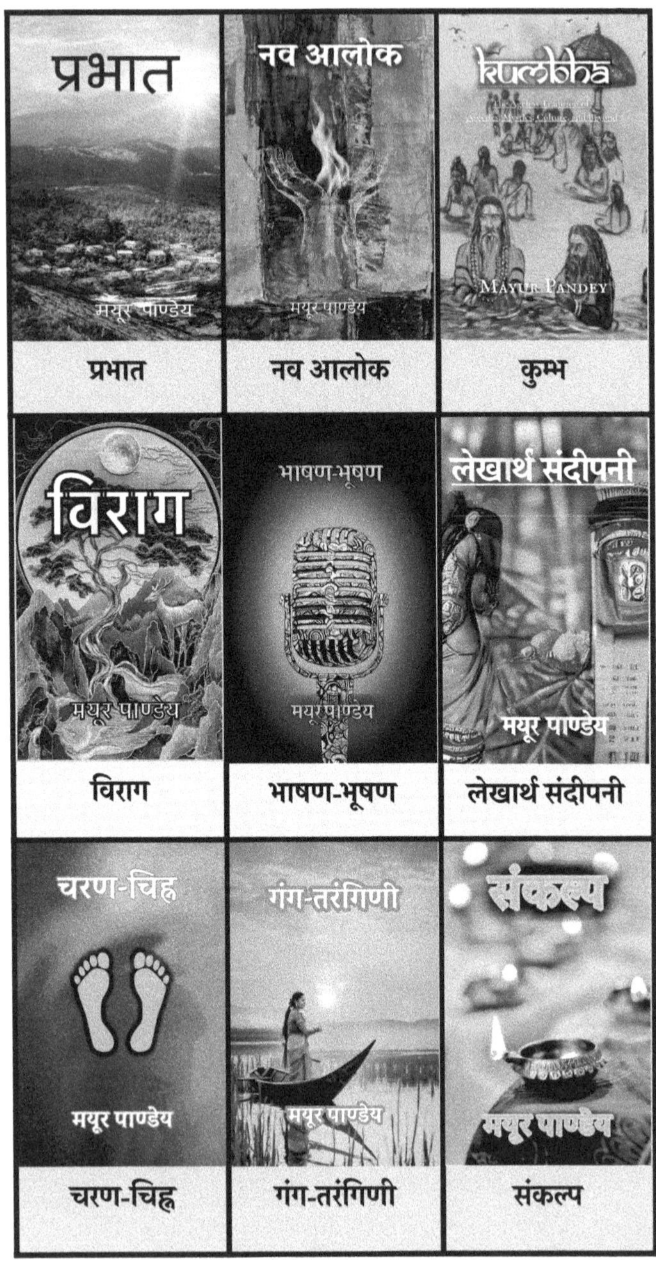

प्रभात	नव आलोक	कुम्भ
विराग	भाषण-भूषण	लेखार्थ संदीपनी
चरण-चिह्न	गंग-तरंगिणी	संकल्प

KUMBHA